PRAISE FOR STEVE BRAUNIAS

FISH OF THE WEEK

'Braunias has intelligently wormed his way into my heart, stirred me
with his gentle eloquence, bowled me with his wit ...'
Matt Rilkoff, *Taranaki Daily News*

'Braunias is one of those clever writers able to deliver brilliant humour
but also to be serious and thoughtful as required'
Graham Beattie, *Beattie's Book Blog*

ROOSTERS I HAVE KNOWN

'Razor-sharp portraits from New Zealand's funniest and most merciless
columnist ... A brilliant and eccentric collection'
Philip Matthews, *Your Weekend*

'Surely our gutsiest journalist ... He sniffs out our social tics, moral bald
spots and obfuscatory nonsense'
Claire Finlayson, *NZ Life & Leisure*

'Provocative, literate, disrespectful ... eminently readable'
Christopher Moore, *The Press*

'Braunias proves he is our best newspaper feature writer'
Warwick Roger, *North & South*

HOW TO WATCH A BIRD

'Braunias has touchingly brought together love and bird-watching in
a book that stalks sewage ponds and grey warblers with curiosity and
affection, and ends with contentment, bliss and a baby born'
NZ Listener: Best Books of the Year

'A revelation'
John McCrystal, *Herald on Sunday*

'Braunias is himself a rare bird ... he illuminates our homes like no other'
David Geary, *Scoop*

STEVE BRAUNIAS

SMOKING IN ANTARCTICA
SELECTED WRITING

AWA PRESS

First edition published in 2010 by Awa Press,
16 Walter Street, Wellington 6011, New Zealand.

The columns and articles in this book originally appeared in
The Sunday Star-Times.

The right of Steve Braunias to be identified as the author of
this work in terms of Section 96 of the Copyright Act 1994
is hereby asserted.

National Library of New Zealand Cataloguing-in-Publication Data
Braunias, Steve.
Smoking in Antarctica : selected writing / by Steve Braunias.
ISBN 978-1-877551-11-6
1. Braunias, Steve. 2. New Zealand — Social conditions.
3. New Zealand—Social life and customs. I. Title.
070.92—dc 22

Cover photograph by Jane Ussher
Cover design by Spencer Levine
Typeset by Jenn Hadley
Printed by McPherson's Printing Group, Australia
This book is typeset in Fournier, Frutiger and Stag.

www.awapress.com

ABOUT THE AUTHOR

Steve Braunias writes a weekly column in
The Sunday Star-Times, and his articles are syndicated
in newspapers across New Zealand. A frequent speaker at
conferences and writers' festivals, he has written for TV
series *Eating Media Lunch*, and has been awarded a Montana
Book Award, fellowships to both Oxford and Cambridge
universities, and the Buddle Findlay Sargeson Fellowship,
and has won over 20 national writing awards. He was
appointed editor in residence at the Waikato Institute of
Technology in 2010. He lives in Auckland with his family.
This is his fifth book.

**E. delivered of a son.
Received green swallow from Jamaica.**

Edmund Gosse, *Father and Son* (1907)

To E and M

Contents

FATHER'S DAYS

THE STATE WE'RE IN

THE NATIONAL STOMACH

Introduction:
A Brief History of Happiness

These are the finest times of my life. The two years covered in this selection of writings – 2008 to 2010 – already stare back at me like a series of cheerful postcards sent from a land of myth. I flew to Antarctica and found the strangest smoking deck in the world. I commuted by train to the even more far-flung and far-fetched destination of Hamilton. I climbed the stairs of a tree hut in Auckland's Albert Park and attempted to write a novel. But most of the time I stayed at home, adoring and agog, as the capital city of my life took on a new, complex shape. I was like all parents of young children. I fell wildly in love with my daughter every day.

She doubled her age overnight. She turned two years old, and celebrated her birthday by running naked in the backyard with her cousins. She turned three years old, and celebrated her birthday by running naked in the backyard with her cousins. Her reliable nudity was one of the few constants. All else was revolution.

She has two working parents. Like most couples, we arrange our work around our child. It's the usual whirlwind of the morning shower for us and the bath before bedtime for her, and the dishes and the dollies and the sobbing demands. It's happiness. It's everything. But how strange it is, with every passing day, to know that we'll never see her again. That fat-cheeked lump, dazed and incapable of a civilised conversation, who was taken home from the maternity ward to sleep in a bassinet in our bedroom – gone, lost. An ex-baby. The one-year-old and two-year-old, too, are ancient history. Children disappear. It's the greatest magic act in the history of the world. They do it right in front of your nose but you never see it happening until the rabbit is out of the hat and is dressing itself. The columns about her here are backstage reports.

After the birth of his children, C.K. Stead wrote in a poem: 'I do not want my life back.' The question is how to manage the rest of it. I'm too busy being a happy parent to know whether I'm a good parent, and how does anyone measure that? The least you can do is provide. My daughter was born in February 2007. I quit my job at Christmas that year to stay home and look after her while my fiancée returned to full-time work. I continued to write my weekly column, and sometimes accepted other assignments. I thought of myself as semi-retired; officially, and with hilarious timing, I was unemployed just as the recession moved its way towards New Zealand.

Waiting for it to wash up on our shores was like a throwback to the time we had to wait three months for supplies to reach us by ship from England. In the 1970s, football mad and growing up in Mount Maunganui, I stalked Mr Bates' bookshop in Central Parade every Monday for the latest *Shoot!*, *Goal* and *World Soccer* magazines. Now and then I'd save enough money to buy special deliveries of the *Daily Mirror*. Monday to Saturday editions of the newspaper were held together in a bright, gluey yellow binding, and shipped out to the Commonwealth. The marvellous absurdity is that my bounty of the latest magazines and the morning paper were three months out of date. I waited that long for old news.

For at least that long in 2008, New Zealand waited for bad news. The recession — at first it was called 'the credit crunch', which didn't sound too injurious — swept across the US. It travelled to Britain and Europe. Iceland sank in its path. To what extent would it bend New Zealand out of shape? If the suspense didn't kill you, maybe the reality of it would.

Was there ever a bubble? All most of us knew was that it had burst; the mood of the country became so disgruntled that few could remember a time when we were happily gruntled. To help make ends meet, many got out a spade and turned their backyards into market gardens. I turned to Home Brand, and stocked up large on the cut-price range of food at my local supermarket. I became mesmerised by the sight of all those tins with red lettering on white labels. Home Brand wholegrain mustard, Home Brand pickled onions, Home Brand fruit chutney, Home Brand pear halves, Home Brand sultanas, Home Brand sliced beetroot, Home

Brand scotch fingers – I reached the bottom of the barrel when I reached for a packet of Home Brand dehydrated peas.

And so the downside of the finest times of my life is that they were conducted during the rumours and then the facts of an economic slump. I thought: oh well. Later, I thought: oh dear. Fatherhood and much else began to take on a different hue. New Zealand, too, began to change. A siege mentality came into place. People said the thing to do was keep your head down. I felt the challenge was to keep your head.

The recession was described often enough as a dark cloud overhead, but I felt it in the air at eye level – a kind of static, something crackling and alive, and it did not come in peace. I really did wait for the shrill AH-OOOOGA! blasting out of emergency sirens, and then the announcement: 'Stay in your houses. Do not open the windows.'

For some reason I always expected this to happen whenever I was on Auckland's Great North Road. Much of Great North Road is intense with traffic, and not merely at rush hour. I stood on the sidewalk and watched cars in their thousands, maybe tens of thousands, roar towards either oblivion or Glenfield. I thought: this is an important moment in history. I thought of it as end days. I was quite possibly failing to meet the challenge of keeping my head.

Statistics measured the dismal reality of job losses and mortgagee sales. I read a story about China's unemployed leaving the cities and wandering in their tens of thousands, maybe hundreds of thousands, across the countryside. Would they pitch up in Glenfield? My primary sources of anxiety were Antarctica and a book published in 1721.

The two went together. I filched a copy of Daniel Defoe's *A Journal of the Plague Year* from a hut overlooking a frozen sea in the Antarctic. I travelled to the blank continent in the summer of 2009 with photographer Jane Ussher on assignment for *North & South* magazine. It was a rare and amazing opportunity, but I can always be relied on to not rise to the occasion. I received Antarctica as a promise of hell. I thought: oh, so this is how life ends. Every second felt like death. On an overnight field exercise with young dungareed men and women from the RNZAF 40 Squadron, an instructor handed out shovels and told us to sculpt an ice cave; I dug a grave.

I spent all that week preoccupied with death. It was the only subject in town. Antarctica was stiff as a board, had long surrendered to total collapse. The most likely diagnosis is that it had been given a terrible shock, and turned white as a sheet. As such, I was in the market for a really good book about the annihilation of mankind.

I found it when stationed in a hut that allowed intimate access to the sensational and grotesque butchery performed by South Polar skuas upon a colony of Adélie penguins. Defoe's book is a record of the sensational and grotesque disease spread by the bubonic plague of 1665. Death carts, church bells, fear. 'When anyone bought a joint of meat in the market they would not take it off the butcher's hand, but took it off the hooks. On the other hand, the butcher would not touch the money, but have it put into a pot full of vinegar.' Theatre and public feasts were prohibited. So was the innocent pastime of bear-baiting. A man with a superb name – Solomon Eagle – took to the streets. 'He went about denouncing judgement upon the city in a frightful manner, sometimes quite naked, and with a pot of burning charcoal on his head.' Was he a contemporary columnist?

There were fears of another plague, in London, in 1721. Defoe's book was intended as a warning. I took it to heart in 2009, in the New Zealand colony, when recession flu was followed by swine flu.

The timing of it was audacious. Hadn't we suffered enough? Answer: no. The story may be apocryphal, but journalist Bill Ralston likes to tell of Muldoon making some cutting remark to a political opponent whose career was already in tatters, and being asked whether that wasn't kicking a man when he was down. Muldoon had replied: 'What better time to do it?' Swine flu arrived just as New Zealand, laid low by the recession, had climbed into its sickbed. This time the emergency AH-OOOOGA! sirens really did blare, from the TV news, which presenters all but read behind a face mask. And was that a copy of *A Journal of the Plague Year* on their desk?

History was in the making. End days were upon us.

I vowed to record it, week in, week out: the columnist as apocalypse correspondent. But I wrote only a handful of feverish despatches. I was distracted by a book. I read it very slowly, because I wrote it very slowly.

I applied for a writers' residency as the Buddle Findlay Sargeson Fellow and got it. That was the easy part. I took up rooms in the treetops of Albert Park, in the Sargeson Centre, and set to fulfilling the promise I made in my application: writing a novel. After a lifetime in journalism, fiction represented a sudden departure. Journalism is a kind of active plagiarism, dependent on the lives of others; fiction establishes its own facts, quotes its own characters. I suffered in style and comfort. The fellowship allowed a generous stipend and the run of the Albert Park apartment for five months. They were the happiest five months of my writing life.

In essence I got nowhere, although it threatened to go somewhere. I wrote over 30,000 words, about half of a first draft. I remember the sheets of paper I pinned to the wall above my fold-out cot – I ticked off chapters, kept a running score of the word count, set goals. The sheets represented mathematical certainties. All else was the maddening uncertainties of language and narrative. I paced, slept, wrote, sat with my head in my hands; the rooms were so quiet and beautiful, and I adored Albert Park. In summer, the sidewalk across the street smelled of ginkgo trees. In autumn, I squeezed myself through a skylight, and watched the tender light of late afternoons from a perch on the roof. In winter, grapefruit appeared on a tree in the park, and it was time to leave.

I left the city behind. Although the Albert Park apartment was in the trees, it was a downtown address, right beside the CBD. I wandered and explored at night, and can report that downtown Auckland is full of Asians. It's entirely possible someone else has noticed that. But, even in their numbers, they were a tribe outside the New Zealand tribe. Who knew what they were saying? Who even knew who they were? Semi-transient, staring from apartment balconies that had only enough room for a pot plant and a flimsy, foldable clothes horse, they were nameless in New Zealand. My discovery of scattered business cards one night in Albert Park was like a puzzle with too few clues. It became obvious they belonged to a young Asian woman, but who? And was she all right? There was probably an innocent explanation, but I thought back to the missing cards when another, awful discovery was made in 2010: the body of murdered Auckland student Jiayi Li, eighteen, in the boot of an abandoned car in Hamilton.

Missing persons, missing city: much of downtown Auckland felt deserted. The windows of empty shops and dark apartments were festooned with large notices that read: TO LEASE. There was always a number to ring and very often the name was someone called Mohammed. Did anyone ever call? Sometimes I wondered about phoning him just so he could hear a human voice.

It suited my mood to sometimes pick my way through the damp, dreamy grounds and gardens of old Government House, and sit in on murder trials at High Court. There was the one about the prostitute who murdered her former boyfriend after he told her he'd had sex with other prostitutes. Every murder trial is a detailed catalogue of wretchedness and sadness. In the Crown v. Dionne Neal, it included the cup of tea the victim had made for his girlfriend in his Parnell flat, before she killed him with a really long knife and later told police, 'It was like stabbing a roast.'

Her trial was in May. In June and July, all of New Zealand sat in on a murder trial in Dunedin. It became a public spectacle. The timing of it – in the middle of winter, in the middle of the recession – provided New Zealand with a tangible enemy. It wore glasses and a beard, and it snickered. After the complexities regarding the guilt or innocence of David Bain, Scott Watson and Mark Lundy, here was something so completely unambiguous that it brought the nation together. The fear and loathing was a shared experience. It was as though it cast a spell. Everyone went under it. It was called Weatherston.

Clayton Weatherston killed Sophie Elliott. He pleaded not guilty. His defence was provocation. He would have stood a better chance by arguing for insanity, like that flatulent wretch Antonie Dixon, who also went berserk with a blade in his hands. But Weatherston's entire cause on the witness stand was to call for reason. All of New Zealand watched him in court on TV; all of New Zealand found his argument profoundly unacceptable, and Weatherston profoundly intolerable. The jury did the rest, and found him guilty.

'Everyone', 'all', 'the nation' – but there was at least one dissenting voice. A man called Paul emailed after my column about Weatherston. Paul wrote:

'Thirty years ago I had a relationship with someone. We lived together, broke up, then there was a two-year period of "maybe getting back together". During this time there was an endless series of interactions that made me very, very angry. I would be in a bar or restaurant, and if she was there and I went up to say "Hi" I was treated like dirt. If I didn't, her friends would come up to me and say she was in the back crying because I was ignoring her.

'Get the picture? Multiply that by a hundred times. Finally I went to see a therapist and said, "She's driving me crazy. What is wrong with me that I just can't walk away from it?" After describing all the stuff that she did and said, the therapist made the observation: "Paul, that's how people get themselves killed."

'And while I had no such thoughts, I remember thinking at the time, you know, if I did such a thing and explained what I went through to the jury, they would pretty well let me off.

'Of course no one deserves to die – especially as Ms Elliott did – but consider this. They were two seemingly pleasant people, but in their relationship she was a manipulative, abusive lunatic. She drove him crazy and he snapped. But all we hear from the papers was that she was a saint and he was a psycho.'

I took his email seriously. Like Paul, I developed an intense dislike for the media's infantile need to create two stock characters – the heroine and the villain. It played to the lynch mob. But all that was after the fact. You couldn't really move beyond that fact. It was a higher mathematic. The fact was that Clayton Weatherston took a knife to Sophie Elliott, and stabbed her 216 times.

Recession, swine flu, Weatherston – but good news was always at hand in the shape of John Key. This book includes the 2008 election campaign. Everyone knew the result was a done deal. Key smiled his way into office. He was a man too relaxed to bother with vowels; the way he spoke was like a labour-saving device. If it seemed the only thing inside his head was thin air, a fascinated nation walked around inside that vacant lot, disarmed by its roominess and space. Everything about him was taken in good spirit. He represented a kind of wholesome decency – happiness, health, and considerable personal wealth.

Key lived with his wife and two children in a gated mansion; he joked about digging up the tennis court to plant vegetables. Labour's leader, Helen Clark, owned a modest villa with her meek professorial husband; a magnet held a list of their household chores on the fridge – whose turn was it to buy Home Brand dehydrated peas? The one time the election campaign broke a sweat was when Clark tripped and fell face-first on the floor at the Riccarton shopping mall. She was still there when Key accepted the applause on election night.

In any case Labour were as much use as a busted clock, and New Zealand First leader Winston Peters looked sleepless and haggard: the media kept setting his alarm, and he spent his last remaining months in power trying to turn it off, fumbling in the dark to silence the ringing of one scandal after another. He was right to exhibit a persecution complex. But he made a lousy martyr: it was difficult to see if he had a cause beyond staying in power. The ordeal turned him into a dreadful neurotic. He was dead man barking mad.

Key remains a stranger to mental health issues. He just gets on with it. For much of his first term, New Zealand has had its hands full keeping the wolf from the door; it hasn't had time to stop and discuss the finer details. Key is the power that loves our vacuum. But it's harsh to continue thinking of him as an empty vessel, a weightless balloon. He displays sound management skills. He's decisive. Long before he faces his first election challenge, even his harshest critics acknowledge Key as New Zealand's greatest prime minister since Helen Clark.

There was a time when I harboured an ambition to report on politics and parliament as a journalist in the press gallery.

The time lasted from 1.14 p.m. to 1.17 p.m. one lackadaisical afternoon. The great workings of political process take place in shadowy corners, and the challenge is to wave a torch until the beam strikes something that moves. But one of my prime interests as a columnist is to illuminate various aspects of New Zealand life that stare us in the face. You could say I very often shine light on things that are already completely visible in broad daylight.

As a fantasist who thinks he's on to something, I make it my business to read the writing on the wall, and I began to realise in 2009 that it was really badly spelled: it led to a series of columns on the comic misspellings of shop signs and other public notices.

It was good fun while it lasted, but it didn't last long. Instead of celebrating the anarchy of language, too many readers condemned it, and surrendered to the great New Zealand pastime: complaint. Scarcely a week goes by in the press without some headline writer stencilling: WATCH-DOG BODY CALLS FOR HIGHER STANDARDS. But there is so much inventiveness and original thinking in low standards. This was evident when I wrote another series of columns on the comic tradition of really bad New Zealand meals.

The most elevated aspect of New Zealand life are birds. They stare us in the face. They scatter their brilliance in the sky. Strange to think they go about their business while remaining unaware of the intense fascination they inspire in

New Zealand's affiliate of birders. One of the most exhilarating days of 2009 was travelling to a field in Takanini, south Auckland, to see the rare Franklin's gull. Birders had been raving about its sighting for weeks. It was only the second recorded sighting of the so-called American prairie dove in New Zealand. It was lost. Finding it was a giddy feeling. I remember the day and the moment – cold and grey and blustery, the wind moving across an ugly sportsfield, puddles of rain, and there, delicate and alive, a small, good thing, the Franklin's gull.

I felt a similar leap of the heart when I saw a street sign that read: GOVERNOR FITZROY PLACE. Again, the day and the moment remain vivid, fixed – an idle amble in the morning sun in downtown Auckland, on my way to the Sargeson Centre for another day of discovery and misery, and then craning my neck to gape, open-mouthed, at the little tin sign which revealed the name of my favourite character in New Zealand history. Poor FitzRoy! New Zealand's second governor was chased out of town in 1845. He returned to London. Misbegot and woebegone, he took his own life. But he had been a man of courage and no little genius. The street sign was a minor recognition – it had been put up a couple of years earlier, without comment – but it felt good to have him back in Auckland, in New Zealand, in broad daylight.

Later, I walked the length of the street. It's not a very long length. It took about five minutes, but I spent a couple of hours inside two of the buildings – a Mormon institute

14

and an art gallery. By weird and moving serendipity, the gallery's latest exhibition included a duplication of a nineteenth-century lithograph that featured FitzRoy. The past and the present came together: FitzRoy on Fitzroy Place.

It presented a vision. I saw a book. A book about FitzRoy in New Zealand today. I looked up every place in New Zealand named after him. They included Fitzroy Beach in New Plymouth, the suburb Fitzroy in Hamilton, Fitzroy Steps on Bluff Hill in Napier, Port Fitzroy on Great Barrier Island, and Fitzroy Bay near Eastbourne, Wellington. I would visit each place and write about it as it is now, and tie in haunting biographical material. The past and the present would come together in thrilling, original harmony. Fantastic! The deadline was fast approaching for a writers' award that every year hands out two prizes of $35,000 for a non-fiction project. Perfect! I hurried off an application. Strangely, other writers were chosen.

I put the disappointment aside. I also put the novel aside. As much as I wanted to starve my family and live off the smell of a Home Brand oily rag, I gave up my literary pretensions and came out of semi-retirement. I'm back on Grub Street. At least I still have literary allusions. The reference to George Gissing's 1891 novel *New Grub Street* – the story of men and women forced to write for a living – was used as a headline in a series of columns about my career as a media and literary nobody. But I'm a nobody with range. I write satires for various publications every week, and occasionally choose an unsuspecting New Zealand town to pester in a photo essay with Jane Ussher. I appear in televised debates in front of a vaguely live audience, and often amble onstage at literary festivals. I give keynote speeches at conferences, and mentor journalism students at Hamilton's Waikato Institute of Technology in my pompous title as editor in residence.

I do it for fun and I do it for income. It's also true that the engagements are a running away from the fear of failure: I didn't finish the novel because I was afraid it was absolute rubbish. At best, I was afraid it was semi-absolute rubbish. Fear has dragged me back down to the rough trade of journalese and columnese. It's probably where I belong. I'm happy with my address on Grub Street.

A novel has a chance of lasting. The point of journalism is its obsolescence: it's built to fade. Is there some kind of presumption of permanence in selecting columns to reappear between the covers of a book? Possibly. I never saw a delusion of grandeur that I didn't like. But when I look back on the two years of my life and other people's times as recorded here, I also look back on writing a column every week since 1999. At the age of three, my daughter asked: 'What's a column, Dad?' I love her questions. I gave some prosaic reply. Darling, I should have said, it's my life's work.

POLITICS

Tea at Devonport

G ibbon famously viewed history as 'little more than the register of the crimes, follies and misfortunes of mankind'. As parliament prepares to wind up for the year and despatch MPs to face the bracing or fetid air of the campaign trail, I thought it might be instructive to consult a particular register of history: the *Hansard* journals of 1908.

A century ago, New Zealand went to the polls in similar conditions – a long-term, fundamentally left-wing government up against a conservative opposition. There may be other likenesses. Michael Bassett described Joseph Ward's ruling Liberal Party thus: 'While the economy prospered, Ward's government lacked clear direction. Bold promises of legislation would be lost in controversy, retraction, prevarication and paralysis.' But there is a more exact parallel between the opposition leaders of 1908 and 2008. According to a contemporary historian, Ward's rival, Bill Massey, 'never had an original idea in his life'.

What were the profound issues, the matters of great import, as recorded in *Hansard* a hundred years ago? Members discussed the best way to burn diseased potatoes. They pondered the necessity of issuing free schoolbooks to

'Natives'. They also debated one of the central questions of non-existence: how can you tell when someone is dead?

A report was tabled. It read: 'The question of premature burial of our fellow creatures is a matter which has agitated the public mind at Home.' There were 219 cases of 'escape from premature burial' in England; they included an elderly gentleman who sat up in his coffin just as it was about to be screwed down. Members said they had heard tell of similar stories in Kawhia, Rotorua and Palmerston North – even then, it was hard to tell the living from the dead in Palmerston North.

It was suggested that every death should be pronounced only 'after having tested the radial artery'. This was spelled out as cutting the artery to see if blood flowed from it. Members worried about the expense. Sir Walter Carncross thought it was worth it. He rose to make a magnificent speech. 'We may owe the flattering unction,' he said, 'to our souls that these cases of premature burial are very few. But it is impossible to know how many there are, because in most cases the unfortunate victim is coffined up.'

There was a spirited debate on the Quackery Prevention Bill. One of the Hutt Valley's greatest sons, Thomas Wilford, a theatrical courtroom orator, provincial rugby representative, and life member of the Wellington Boxing Association, regarded doctors as no better than crooks who peddled snake oil. 'Doctors are the luckiest men in the world,' he said. 'When they make a success, the whole world triumphs in it, and when they make a failure, the earth covers it up.'

The ludicrous member for Wairarapa, John Hornsby, replied: 'That is a shocking libel.'

'Was it?' asked Wilford.

'Yes.'

Wilford said he was sorry to hear it.

'The honourable member should be ashamed to say it.'

Wilford said, 'It does not worry me.'

Hornsby was up on his feet again to debate the most hotly contested issue of 1908: tea rooms. As the law stood, it was illegal for anyone to sell a cup of tea on a Sunday. A woman who ran a tea room at the Devonport wharf had been prosecuted. Was this fair and right? Yes, said Hornsby.

Allowing the sale of tea on a Sunday, he said, 'would be a bad thing for the country, as it had been a very evil thing for many other countries.' Sunday was a day of rest. No one ought to work.

Francis Fisher of Wellington Central asked Hornsby what he was planning to do on Sunday.

'I am going to church.'

All Sunday?

'Not the whole day.'

What might he do when not in church?

'I have made no arrangements.'

Fisher then asked Hornsby what advice he would give to families wishing to stop in at a tea room on a Sunday for a cup of tea, and even, he wildly surmised, a slice of cake.

Hornsby: 'They can walk around the bays.'

Hornsby was insane but he was not a lone voice. Auckland West MP Charles Poole commented, 'I offer no apology for expressing the anxiety to see the seventh day kept as quietly as possible by the people of this Dominion, in their own interests.'

Ward declared the House adjourned for the year at 12.10 a.m. on October 10. He wished everyone luck in the coming election. So did Massey. He said, 'We are entering upon our usual triennial fight, and I can only express the hope that, after it is over, we shall be able to come back and shake hands and be as good friends as we are now.' He eventually succeeded Ward, bringing to an end the Liberals' fortunate experiment of social equality in New Zealand. Ever onwards, confirming Gibbon's diagnosis.

[September 14, 2008]

The Old Campaigner

He realised the second he woke up that he was lying straight in his bed. The media ought to be here to see this, he thought. But even when presented with the evidence they probably wouldn't believe it, or bother to inform the public of what was an indisputable fact. Those morons, those sacks of shit! They called him such terrible names.

It was going to be another busy day, but he allowed himself the indulgence of his morning ritual. He stared at his reflection in the mirrored ceiling, admired the set of his mouth, the firm jaw, the soulful eyes. His hair, powerful and magnificent, loomed above the pillow like Everest. These glad sights entertained him for an hour.

Reluctantly, he climbed out of bed in his beautifully tailored three-piece pinstriped pyjama suit. He had worn it last night when he gave his speech to a Grey Power audience. They were too old to notice that the material was flannel. It had been a long, tiring day; the pyjama suit allowed him to go to bed without needing to change.

It was the kind of tactic that gave him an edge on the campaign trail. He knew all the tricks. He was experienced, seasoned, a veteran. He reflected on this as he sipped at his tea. He had given so many years of public service, devoted himself to so many selfless causes. It had made him a legend in his own lifetime. He smiled; he was like the man in the joke about standing next to the Pope: 'Who's the guy in the white hat?'

He looked at his watch. 6.38 a.m. Good. An early start to the day. He gripped the sides of his armchair to get up, but then he wondered: what day is it? He couldn't remember. He sat down again, and poured himself more tea. He held the cup with both hands as he brought it to his mouth. He closed his eyes... He woke to the sound of his mobile phone. He looked at his watch. 9.14 a.m. Incredible. He snatched at his phone and looked at the screen. A name came up: Garner. Fuck TV3, he thought, and let the call go.

It would only be another petty inquiry. Garner's booming, smarmy voice asking something like, 'How do you respond to the latest poll which puts you at...' Two percent, one percent – it didn't matter. The only poll that counted was on election day, November 8. But what was today's date? My God, he thought, was it November 8? He held up his phone. Ha. October the something – he didn't bother with the fine print.

He padded across the shag-pile carpet into the kitchen and filled the jug. His feet felt cold on the linoleum. He opened the pantry, and found his slippers. He waited a long time for the water to boil, and stared out the window at the way the morning sunlight fell gently on the leaves of a plane tree...

He looked at his watch. 11.31 a.m. Bother. He glared at the jug, and this time he switched it on.

Settling back in his armchair, he blew on his tea and thought about last night's speech. 'I have enemies ... Their false allegations ... Lies ... Not a shred of evidence.' And: 'Beware of criminals ... Beware of immigrants.' It went well. The audience was warm, supportive, believing – although there was one unpleasant incident. In his speech he described how the media had set about attacking him with one lie after another. 'It reminds me of the old saying, "I shot an arrow into the air. Whither it landed, I knew not where."' At this, a frail and ancient gentleman cried out: 'Well, how careless! I'd stop that at once, if I were you. You could cause an accident. Arrows! At your age. You should be ashamed of yourself.'

The man was removed, shouting: 'Nurse!' Afterwards, a Grey Power member apologised. 'You'll have to forgive poor old Mr Wilson,' he said. 'He's a bit ... you know.'

He knew. But he brooded on poor old Mr Wilson's words. 'At your age': what was that supposed to mean? He was only sixty-three. Plenty of life left in him. He brooded some more, dozed, and looked at his watch. 5.25 p.m. Tsk. His phone told him he had received thirty-seven texts and missed ninety-one calls. Well, they could wait. He put six fish fingers under the grill. The plane trees were soft and smooth in the early evening light.

At his age... He thought of all the Grey Power audiences

he had ever addressed. He saw their shining heads, heard the clacking of their false teeth. They laughed, they cheered, they knitted blue cardigans, always blue. They had been good to him. He enjoyed their company. But were they getting too close? How much distance was there between the stage and the audience? It seemed to be narrowing in this campaign. He felt as though he was being drawn in, clutched at by invisible arms, as they chanted: 'Join us...'

He was back in bed. Wearily, he looked at his watch. 11.07 p.m. Fuck. Tomorrow was another day. But which day? Was it two percent or one percent? Why was Duncan Garner standing next to the Pope? Could this really be the end? He pulled the blankets tighter over his tea-stained, fish-crumbed pyjama suit, and cried out: 'Nurse!'

[October 19, 2008]

The Lady Campaigner

She said to her driver, 'Actually, no. Go along the coast road.' He nodded and turned right at the intersection. They drove until the road ended at a gate. She put away her papers and said, 'Wait here a bit. I need to stretch my legs.' The track was deserted. She thought: no one need ever know that the most powerful woman in New Zealand took time out to walk alongside Wellington harbour in the middle of an election campaign.

There were a million things to do. There was strategy to discuss, policy to shape, a country to run. But it was a lovely spring afternoon. A light breeze pushed her hair behind her ears. The tide sucked in its breath as it fell on the shore. She resolved to walk for just a few minutes. Five. Ten at most.

Sunlight lit the yellow broom and gorse on the hillside. A thin waterfall struggled through the rock; she drank a few fresh, cold drops from her cupped hands. It felt so good. Her shoes scuffed at the hard track, the patterns made by bicycle tyres. ... Her mind had gone blank for thirteen minutes. Thirteen minutes was a long time in politics. Anything could have happened. A leak, a revelation, some damn fool shooting off at the mouth – was Mallard under lock and key?

For a moment, she wondered if she was experiencing something resembling panic. She felt her pulse. Nothing there. Good. Situation normal.

But it was best to make certain everything was going to plan. She prodded at a speed-dial number on her mobile. It went straight to the answering message. Bother. She trudged on, staring beyond the water to the distant outline of the Kaikoura ranges.

She knew by instinct to look at the ranges. Always take the long view. But she began thinking about the long view backwards into the past. She had been in power for nine years. Nine long, good years. History would remember her. How, though? Immortality was a strange business. She had read on Russell Brown's blog that someone had sampled David Lange's Oxford Union speech on to a music track called 'David Lange You Da Bomb'. Well, perhaps that nice Chris Knox would pay her the same compliment. Even one of his records would be better than the error-ridden, clichéd eulogies already being written by the news media.

Eulogies! What was she thinking? Like the petrels she saw in the sky, a word had floated before her: defeat. She flung out a hand as though to scare it off. Defeat wasn't in her vocabulary. She didn't even know what the word meant, and she was damned if she was going to look it up in the dictionary on election day, November 8.

She rang the number again. No answer. What was the woman playing at? The job description she had written contained the instruction, 'To be available at all times of the day and night.' But the woman hadn't been available for the past twenty-five minutes while she had been walking the track. Anything could have happened...

She stopped to look at the kelp writhing on the shore. It made her think of Key. Key, the novice; Key, the hollow man; Key, the barbarian at the gate, confident he was about to assume control and splash his big fat flat kelpy feet all over her desk. What was he saying today? What was there for her to pounce on, sink her teeth into? Once more, she rang the number; once more, the voice said, 'Leave a message.'

For God's sake! She could have the woman fired for this. Or had she already thrown in the towel, given up, quit? Was it possible she was a rat leaving a sinking ship? Now, more than ever, was the time for all hands on deck. As she rounded a bend in the track, she saw the inter-island ferry sailing towards port. Its safe passage calmed her, made her see reason. She could have every faith in the woman's loyalty.

'This one's about trust.' It was a simple and effective campaign message. But who did she trust? Of course there was the woman – her able lieutenant, her most valued adviser. Who else? The black humour which had seen her through so many tough times made her think of Peters. He was his own sinking ship. It would take more than him to drag her down, too, into the depths, the dark, appalling depths...

An hour later, the track led her to an abandoned lighthouse. Beside it was an old shed. She took shelter; the breeze had turned into a sharp southerly. It shrieked in her ears. She thought of the empty, silly slogan, parroted by Key and *The New Zealand Herald* and all the rest of them: 'Winds of change!' It threatened to blow away everything she had built, knock it down like a house of cards. ... Cold, hungry, tired, she leaned against the shed wall, and looked at the light-house. It wasn't a beacon any longer. It was just a relic.

Her phone rang. She looked at the initial that appeared on the screen: H. At last! Compose yourself, she thought. Act nonchalant. Remember who's boss. She picked up the woman's call, and said, 'Heather Simpson ... Oh, hello, Helen. What'd you get on Key this morning?'

[October 26, 2008]

The Winner

He unscrewed his head, placed it on the bedside table, and lay down. 'That's a weight off my shoulders,' he said. But his head floated up and met the ceiling with a thud. 'Ow,' he said. His head bounced down, and then floated up again. 'Ow,' he said.

The sequence continued for some time. He tried to outsmart the ceiling, but without success. He gave the ceiling credit. He viewed it as the toughest opponent he had met these past few weeks on the campaign trail. No one else was putting up much of a fight. The campaign was too easy, a formality. He knew where he would be on election day, November 8. He had ordered three different versions of his victory speech: rare, medium rare and well done, although they all read the same.

'Ow,' he said. He looked down on his body. It was sleeping like a baby. He felt a surge of affection. It was a reliable body, active and obedient, quite willing to stand on its own two feet. It had dragged him out of the gutter, showed him New York and Parnell. It would lead him to the ninth floor of the Beehive. Good body! He wanted to pat it on the head, but present circumstances led him to give up on the idea.

'Ow,' he said. The tedium of pain was interrupted as a faint breeze floated his head through an open window. He skimmed the surface of the swimming pool, and then lifted over the big front gate. He turned to look at the courtyard lined with manicured trees, and wondered when he would able to return to his house, with its sweeping stairwell, its lovely French and Italian decor, its tasteful gilt-framed mirrors. There were serious questions to consider. How long would he remain in exile? Was he doomed to forever hang in the air, a disembodied presence, bloodless and groundless? The sun was shining. 'Nice day for it,' he said.

He soared above the house, swept along by a warm spring breeze, which offered him panoramic views of Auckland. Auckland! So rich in history. It was founded in ... in ... it was founded long ago, by men in waistcoats and whiskers, men who had vision, who laid the foundations. Their names would never be forgotten. They echoed down the ages. He felt a kinship, a bond, with these ancients. Wherever you are now, he thought, go well Fay, go well Richwhite.

But the effort of scholarship tired him. Besides, the past was boring. He always looked to the future. 'Tomorrow is a brighter day,' he said. True, the global economic forecast was bad. It had been bad before, and what happened? Nothing that he could remember. There was always money to be made as long as you put in the hours and showed some initiative. Good government meant leading by example. 'Let's kick away the obstacles,' he said. He wanted to fling out a leg, but present circumstances led him to give up on the idea.

He looked upon the traffic, and spotted a motorcade. Oho, he thought, I bet I know who this is. Sure enough, a woman in red jacket and pants climbed out of the ministerial car when it parked in a busy shopping street. He watched her shake hands, plant awkward kisses, as she moved through the crowd. It was nice being where he was; he couldn't hear her voice. One day, he thought, we should sit down as friends and I'll feed her crumbs from my table.

Poor old trout! She thought she had his number, but no one knew his number. Numbers were his secret language. Numbers were sacred. They separated man from beast. Words went in one ear and out the other; numbers anchored the world, led it to a safe mooring.

'Ow,' he said. His head hit the mast of a yacht in the marina. When he bounced off, he caught a glimpse of a familiar face on the balcony of a waterfront apartment. It was Brash! His old friend, his former mentor, eating alone from a paper plate. 'Don,' he called. Brash looked up. Their eyes met, just for a moment, and then Brash picked up his plate of corned beef, walked inside the sliding glass doors and closed the curtains.

The wretch! But that was politics for you. Trust wasn't a commodity worth trading. As he floated over the harbour and into the gulf, he thought of how little he could trust English, with his habit of talking too loudly in that ridiculous accent at cocktail parties. Who else, though, was qualified to serve as a credible deputy? He refused to brood on the question. It didn't pay to get bogged down in details. He was a big picture kind of guy. The wind carried him far out to sea.

Oh well, he thought, my body will soon wake up, realise that something's amiss – probably when it goes into the bathroom to brush my teeth – and come to the rescue. It had happened many times before. The thing was to relax, and enjoy the journey. 'At the end of the day,' he said, but couldn't think of another cliché to end the sentence. He was hungry. His head hurt. He closed his eyes, and drifted, drifted, drifted...

[November 2, 2008]

The Meaning of Politics

At the height of the election campaign – good luck to all last night's winners – I visited my local tea room and sat down outside at my usual table with my usual order of a ham-and-egg savoury with a cup of black coffee poured straight from the pot. I borrowed a copy of Auckland's morning paper from the counter. Two people arrived and sat at the next table.

He grimaced, wore dreadlocks, and pulled at the cuffs of his jersey; she was small and pale, and played with a sugar sachet that she held between her long red fingernails. When he talked, he looked sideways, squirming in his chair. She was loud, and leaned forward. We sat outside the café on a pale spring morning.

He asked, 'So, are you living around here?'

She said, 'Yep. With my dad, actually. He's a cool guy. Really cool. But my mother, don't think I'm weird saying this, I know it sounds ironic because she's a Christian, but it's like she's fucking driving me to drugs. She's putting my recovery in jeopardy. I said to Dad, "I don't want that bitch coming around here." He said, "Don't worry, I've changed the locks."'

'How did you like the programme?'

'I don't have a bad word to say about it, except that it was really really hard facing up to my emotions. Like it was full-on. Really difficult.'

'Heavy scary.'

'Not as scary as when I had my breakdown. I was in psychosis when I was twenty-five, twenty-six.'

John Key was ahead in the polls by a narrowing margin, but well ahead in the newspaper's editorial page. Once again it praised his calmness and his fresh approach, and damned Helen Clark's arrogance and her personal attacks.

The man asked, 'So what made you go straight on the narrow? On the straight and narrow?'

The woman said, 'It was hard. It was terrifying. I just couldn't stop. It was just so addictive. I could stop when I was taking the old speed. That didn't worry me. But the new stuff, I couldn't get off. And then the criminal element came into it.'

'Gangs and that.'

'I didn't have a problem with gangs. But I got busted for robbing a till. Reached in and grabbed a handful of notes. They called the cops, and...'

The noise of a passing motorbike managed to drown out her fog-horned confession. I finished my savoury and lit a cigarette.

The man asked, 'Mind if I smoke?'

She said, 'Can you wait 'til I've gone? I just can't be around anything addictive.'

'Oh. Okay.'

'I have the odd joint now and then.'

'It takes the edge off.'

'But it tires me out, so I go to bed for a lie-down and Dad starts to worry that his daughter is back on the drugs.'

Act was promising to get tough on crime. National and Labour were promising to get tough on the economy. The front page of the business and world sections were about the worldwide economic recession. The share market had collapsed in New York, London, Tokyo, Auckland, everywhere.

The woman said, 'It's best to have a job, get some regular money coming in, and establish sleeping patterns, and do exercise and that.

'You need so much money for drugs. Like now I don't have any money because of being on the dole, so it's not an option.

'I used to work the markets. Sold my own products. But then I went to a party and got DIC'd on the way home and they took away my licence. I couldn't work the stalls at the markets as much, couldn't sell my products as efficiently. Just stuck at home without a car. I actually got very lonely and depressed. And you know what it's like. You go into town and take drugs. That went on for three years.'

Three years: that was the prize that Labour, National and all the rest were chasing. The newspaper panted and woofed with excitement. Helen Clark said, 'With your support, we will continue to serve the people of New Zealand.' John Key said, 'My confidence in New Zealand's future is based on my confidence in everyday New Zealanders.'

The man at the corner table stirred his spoon against the sides of an empty coffee cup and asked, 'So, what brings you up to the shops?'

She said, 'Dad caught a couple of flounder and some snapper this morning and I said, "I'll make us a fish curry for dinner." So I'm going to the supermarket and buying some coconut milk and curry powder, rice and salad.'

'Sounds good. I was just at the Mad Butcher buying some meat. I've got a fridge now.'

'Yeah,' the woman said. 'Having a fridge is good, eh.'

[November 9, 2008]

Mr Opportunity

All through the campaign John Key succeeded in looking like a loose goose. He shoved his hands in his pockets. He shrugged and very nearly slouched. Louche and in no particular rush, just passing through New Zealand as though he were taking a stroll, he presented himself as a harmless sort of rooster, a blithe spirit. The pinstriped suit and handsome pair of black English shoes meant business, but that was something he could conduct at his leisure. He waved away the woes of the world, and chanted: 'Opportunity, opportunity, opportunity.' He never seemed to give any serious thought to anything. He left room on his face only for that happy smile. It made him look like a man standing around a barbecue.

The best lies always have a relationship with the truth. Key's image on the campaign trail played on his natural air of confidence and eagerness, the lightness of his intellect, the way he talks as though one side of his mouth is engaged with chewing a stick of gum. But there were hints and glimpses of something else last week as he slouched towards parliament.

'The truth is that you're an idiot!' he yelled at a heckler

in Christchurch. The previous day, at a school in Otara, he snapped again. While students in a computer class tried to ignore the spectacle of a politician facing up to a media scrum in the middle of their classroom, Key was asked about the secretly taped recording of his deputy leader, Bill English, bagging Barack Obama. He replied, 'I'm not going to get in the mud and roll around with a pig.'

He quickly returned to the safety of a moral high ground, and refused invitations to identify the pig. But it was strange to stand pressed up against Key – it's very warm inside a media scrum – and inspect the bitter little rage that had briefly sparked in his brown bovine eyes. Key performs a limited range of emotions; petulance is well within his reach.

It's a waste of time to wonder what makes Key tick. He doesn't tick. A wander inside his brain might well reveal a great many unemployed cells. But what makes him sweat? As prime minister he will face far sterner challenges to his poise and resolve than he did as leader of the opposition. In cabinet, he will have to roll around with his own pigs.

There is also the rather pressing matter of how to deal with a recession. That subject barely registered in the campaign. He fiddled while the economy burned. 'We're going to invest in the future,' he said. What did that mean? At Southern Cross Campus in Mangere he announced that National would establish specialist 'trade academies' in schools, and had earmarked six million dollars towards the Mangere campus. 'It's about opchontee,' he said.

Opportunity, to return vowels where they belong, was his mantra. Even in his mouth, it sounded more exciting than Helen Clark's message: 'Trust.' He was playing the market ('A brighter future!'); she was selling a kind of old, possibly reliable, state insurance. He talked about tomorrow; she had history on her side. But who wants history? You never know how the past will turn out.

At Mangere, Key's entourage included two unannounced guests, Inga Tuigamala and Michael Jones, who pulled up outside the school gates in a big black Chrysler. 'They approached us,' Key shrugged. The former All Blacks gave him star power – he made sure to invoke their names that night on the TV debate – but they performed other, more valuable roles. They were there to connect with Māori and Pacific Islander populations. They were also there to declare the end of history.

They followed Key from the school to Labour territory – the factory floor of the supermarket chain Progressive Enterprises, a stronghold of the National Distribution Union. There, among the high shelves stocked with Party Corn Nachos and Sour Gummy Mixture, they delivered speeches. They were passionate. They were sincere. They finished sentences with the word 'uh'.

Visitors were handed zip-up safety vests; Jones had pulled his over his head like an All Black jersey. 'We've come to know our good friend John quite well,' he began. 'We can trust John. He wants a better society. ... There's a sense of urgency, uh. We don't want to stay in a dependency mindset. My mum always said to me, 'Be the head, not the tail.' We've done the hard yards. The hard mahi, uh. The backbone of this country, of this great country – the greatest country in the world, we're blessed to live here – is built on you people. You've got to vote with your hearts, uh. But vote smart. We've got to make some changes. God bless you all.'

The crucifix swinging in the front window of the Chrysler, the text by evangelist K.P. Yohannan in the back seat – Jones and Tuigamala were a pair of missionaries.

Earlier that morning, when the school pupils rushed across the playground to meet Key, one kid had asked, 'Are you the president?'

Well, Key had already suggested he was New Zealand's answer to Obama. It was a ridiculous vanity, but it didn't do him any harm: New Zealand's answer to anything is far-fetched. Our version of the inexperienced and driven agent of change may lack vision, charisma, soul, language, intelligence, and the small matter of black ancestry, but what's wrong with that? As he strolled around the country these past few weeks, and appealed with his New Zealand qualities of modesty, ambitiousness and cleanliness, he advertised a calming presence.

He was too smooth for Labour. 'Mr Flip-Flop,' they jeered, but every attack was merely a flop. There was party president Mike Williams, squirming as the TV cameras filmed him at the international airport, having returned from Australia with two sets of luggage – the suitcases under his eyes, and twenty-four kilograms of useless documents that were supposed to reveal that Key was guilty of a grave misdeed. They didn't prove anything except Labour's desperation.

The party's 'Two Johns' television advertising campaign, aimed at showing Key's duplicity, also misfired. The maths were all wrong. There wasn't even one John. He was the invisible man. He cancelled himself out – centre-right, a liberal conservative. What did he stand for? What did he truly think? The questions were an irrelevance.

For the past year, National had accused Labour of running out of ideas. Actually, a popular notion is that Labour had too many ideas – all that social engineering, interfering here, imposing rules and prohibitions there. Key's absence of any discernible philosophy, his blank canvas, was a relief from Labour's incessant nation-building. A rest was as good as a change.

His blameless existence, his pleasant torpor, helped take the heat out of the campaign. In the TV debate on Wednesday night, he laughed at how a school kid had once said to him, 'I know who you are. You're Helen Clark's boyfriend.'

Key said, 'That's one thing I'm not!' But it was hard to tell. At the least, National's borrowing of Labour policy suggested a crush.

Divisions were old hat – they belonged to the 2005 election, Clark versus Brash, with a chaotic background starring

Nicky Hager, Bob Clarkson, the Exclusive Brethren, and private detectives allegedly rooting around in rubbish bins. This time around, not even Winston Peters was able to cause a ruckus. His television commercials made you wonder whether he had been filmed on the whispering lawns of a retirement home; the poor devil looked like a garden gnome.

The campaign's quiet, restrained atmosphere suited Key. When he stopped in at south Auckland last week, supported by all the brown faces (MP Tau Henare, candidates Mita Harris and Sam Lotu-liga, missionaries Jones and Tuigamala) he could muster, he was more than content to make small talk. 'What sort of music do you like?' he asked at the school in Mangere. Answer: Katchafire.

'Okay. Have you heard OpShop? They're very commercial, but I like them...

'What do you do in the weekends?' Answer: shopping.

'Uh-huh. Ever go to the Otara markets?' Answer: nah, Sylvia Park.

Amiable, cheerful, patient, he sloped off to another classroom, where a teacher talked over an educational video about food hygiene and the importance of washing your hands. 'Can you see the bacteria? That can kill you, or someone you're cooking for,' she explained. Key smiled, and then approached a group of boys.

'Does anyone have a weekend job?' Answer: yep, at a supermarket.

'What do they pay you? Twelve bucks an hour? Fair enough. I used to be a paperboy. Didn't kill me. Okay! See you later...'

And so on, the usual excruciating campaign chit-chat as more and more kids were subjected to pleasant interrogations by the nice man with untrimmed nose hair and an expensive big-arse watch on his wrist. He was doing the hard yards, the mahi. All of it an audition for the country's top job. The real John Key – assuming he exists – now has to stand up. He said he was ambitious for New Zealand. New Zealand, broke and vulnerable, is ambitious for John Key. He has been granted the opportunity of a lifetime.

[November 9, 2008]

A Brief History of
Sir Roger Douglas

The amazing return of Sir Roger Douglas to parliament will surely see him achieve the status of the greatest politician of modern times. By coincidence, he is already the greatest politician of ancient times. The following is intended as a useful guide for younger readers who may know Sir Roger only as some old guy with a deranged look in his eyes.

One of his most famous appearances in history is recorded in Matthew, when Jesus evicted the money changers from the temple. 'But it's a very favourable rate,' Douglas objected. Jesus responded by overturning his table, and spilling his ink pots. For many years, Douglas remained nostalgic for his currency exchange booth, and vowed to return.

He very nearly passed into legend after King Arthur recognised his services to land reform and invited him to join the Knights of the Round Table. But he was blocked by Lancelot, who had Marxist sympathies. Douglas formed a splinter group. That splinter is now a holy relic, and is worshipped today by the Knights of the Business Roundtable.

Egyptologists have identified Douglas as a recurring figure who features on the tombs of numerous kings. He is usually painted with an arrow through his head. This may have something to do with his advice to Tutankhamen to sell off the pyramids.

The historian George Grote wrote of Alexander the Great: 'All his great qualities were fit for use only against enemies, in which category, indeed, were numbered all mankind.' But Douglas, who served as a junior clerk in the Emperor's accounts department, notes that Alexander often inspired periods of economic prosperity, and has the ledgers to prove it. He was made redundant after Alexander's death, and his job applications were turned down by all mankind.

'Lend me your ears,' said Mark Anthony. Douglas was put in charge of the borrowing programme. He is credited with the adage: 'In the kingdom of the deaf, the one-eared man is king.' He was later interviewed at length when Gibbon came to write *The History of the Decline and Fall of the Roman Empire*.

He returned to Rome as an adviser to the murderous and insane Cesare Borgia, who Douglas recalls as 'not a bad sort of rooster'. He was present when Borgia made his famous recovery after being poisoned. Douglas watched as Borgia wrapped himself in the still quivering carcass of a newly disembowelled mule to overcome the shiverings brought on by fever, and then jumped into a tub of iced water. It saved his life. Douglas immediately scrapped the health system and gave every household a mule. After Borgia's death, he was run out of town on a jackass.

'After his first victory,' writes Douglas's old friend Gibbon of Genghis Khan, 'he placed seventy cauldrons on the fire, and seventy of the most guilty rebels were cast headlong into the boiling water.' Douglas argued that seventy cauldrons was a waste of state expenditure, and presented Khan with a detailed report. 'We should look at the options and possibilities of contracting out cauldrons to private firms. ... Where this has been done by central and local government, savings of thirty percent plus have been achieved,' he told Khan. Douglas was applauded for his initiative and placed in charge of establishing a chain of Mongolian barbecue restaurants. It went into receivership.

Douglas signed on with Columbus as chief petty cash officer when he set sail for America on August 3, 1492. He treated Columbus to readings from his book, *Just Do It*. 'Teenage violence, young mothers, welfare dependency, graffiti, disdain for authority, it's all around us. ... Hard work increases personal freedom. ... The fact is that many individuals must be allowed to fail and feel the results of their failure. Only when they understand that and want to help themselves will we be able to help them help themselves...' He was put ashore on August 4, 1492.

He enjoyed longer service at sea when he sailed with Cortés in 1518. William Prescott writes in his book *History of the Conquest of Mexico*: 'Cortés was avaricious, yet liberal; bold to desperation, yet cautious and calculating in his plans; magnanimous, yet very cunning; courteous and affable in his deportment, yet inexorably stern; lax in his notions of morality, yet (not uncommon) a sad bigot.' Cortés and Douglas got on famously. When they returned from their voyage, Douglas recruited him into his political party but they fell out after Cortés changed his name to Hide.

Douglas made his last voyage when he signed on with Cook in 1769. He assumed the role of land purchaser. When the *Endeavour* approached Poverty Bay, he advised, 'Demonstrate to iwi how privatisation will lead to greater efficiency as a result of a more open and competitive marketplace, and then sell it.' When they landed in the Bay of Islands, he advised: 'Ensure iwi are kept fully informed about foreign ownership, employment opportunities, and price, and then sell it.' When they reached the South Island, he advised: 'Oh, just sell it.' But Cook wouldn't listen. He made noises about the benevolent state. Douglas disappeared into the wilderness. For many years, he remained nostalgic for the country of his youth and vowed to return.

[November 30, 2008]

THIS WRITING LIFE

Paul Theroux in New Zealand

Poor, stupid, cringing, anxious, resentful, thin-lipped and frowning New Zealand, always prepared to carry a grudge, never willing to forgive and forget. Why do we behave like that in front of visitors? Do we behave like that?

I have just finished reading *Ghost Train to the Eastern Star*, the latest travel book by Paul Theroux, in which he retraces the journey he took over thirty years ago when he wrote his first travel book, *The Great Railway Bazaar* – from London to Europe to India to South-east Asia to Japan to Russia and back to Waterloo Station, by train, by rickshaw, by tuk-tuk, always with his feet near the ground as he passes by with his notebook and a preferred brand of ballpoint pen. Near the end of the book he meets another travel writer, Pico Iyer, and they talk about New Zealand.

It's a wonderful book. So many of the best non-fiction writers – Andrew O'Hagan, Joan Didion, Gore Vidal, Jonathan Raban, Graham Greene, W.G. Sebald, Theroux – are novelists. There is a boring notion that Theroux is a grouch, a curmudgeon, but this is insulting because it limits the depth and purpose of his travel books. *Ghost Train* is a wise, tender, enormously funny book, written with a novelist's respect for character and place, and the forward motion of his journey – always on the move, in depressing Romania, appalling Turkmenistan, gorgeous Sri Lanka, infantilised Singapore, and so on – gives it a natural kind of narrative momentum.

It's also a lonely book. Theroux travels alone; all his travel books are lonesome. In *Ghost Train* he seizes an opportunity to yap with his friend Iyer, who lives in Japan.

Earlier, Theroux hangs out with another writer, Haruki Murakami, in Tokyo. I interviewed Murakami four years ago at his Tokyo apartment; he's a strange, thoughtful, quiet sort of rooster, and his silences stalk Theroux as they take a voyeur's tour of Pop Life, which houses 'six busy floors' of sex shops.

They retreat to a bar, and Theroux drunkenly tells Murakami of his miserable visit to Tokyo in 1973 – how he waved goodbye to his wife and two sons when he set out on his journey, felt homesick the whole way, and phoned home twice, from New Delhi and Tokyo. 'Why did my endearments sound unwelcome?' The answer: 'I had not been missed. I had been replaced. My wife had taken a lover.' But he moved back home and wrote his book. 'I made the book jolly, and like many jolly books it was written in an agony of suffering.'

Maybe he talked about that worst time of his life to Iyer too, but Theroux records they mostly discussed books. Shop talk, light and energetic. They meet in Kyoto, and then the next day in Nara, where Iyer lives, and walk through

Yoshikien Garden and Deer Park – shrines, hedges, orna-
ments, bridges. It's a relaxing couple of days. Theroux is
relieved to have company. The following dialogue is on page
454:

'I gave a lecture in New Zealand on travel about ten years
ago. Quite a large group of people. When it came time for
questions, a man stood up and said, "Can you tell us about
Paul Theroux's marriage?"'

'Ha! Poor you!'

'I'd flown in from LA. I'd prepared this long talk. I'd
been very conscientious. And that was the first question.'

'New Zealanders are mad at me because I satirised their
governor-general.'

By which Theroux meant his famous description in *The
Happy Isles of Oceania* (1992) of the eating habits of Dame
Cath Tizard. He wrote: 'I caught her grinning at me, but she
was not grinning. She was trying to dislodge a bit of food
that had found its way between her teeth, and, still talking
and grinning, she began picking her teeth. Having freed the
food from her teeth, she glanced at it and pushed it into her
mouth.'

Reaction to the book was savage. Theroux was given a
sound thrashing. 'People who don't read books a lot,' Theroux once told *The Observer*, 'are threatened by books. The
idea of being written about is threatening.' Was that the
case here? Theroux's remark to Iyer – 'New Zealanders are
mad at me' – suggests a bitter little nation, backward and

provincial, still nursing a grievance.

And the man who stood up at Iyer's lecture is cast as nosy and foolish, a time-waster, petty. But the lecture was about travel writing. The beaky Kiwi had asked a good question. *The Happy Isles of Oceania* opened with Theroux announcing that his marriage had just ended. Afloat and astray, he paddled around New Zealand, Australia and the Pacific. In Christchurch he saw a happy family eating dinner in a fried chicken restaurant on Papanui Road, and was moved to tears. He had once known that warmth.

Theroux relives the agony of suffering at his wife's infidelity in *Ghost Train to the Eastern Star.* It catches up with him, and then passes. Older, remarried, happy, he's over it now. He has other things to think about: a whole world.

[August 31, 2008]

Grub Street: On Television

Apparently I was on television the other day. An email set out the date and time for my appearance as a guest bore on *The Good Word*, a series about New Zealand writers and writing, which I gather is broadcast on digital channel 17b.

The interview took place on a hot summer's day just before Christmas. A goose roasting in my black suit, I turned up at the studios and was escorted to the Green Room, where I was presented with a still life of Don McGlashan sitting next to a bunch of grapes. I thought: I'd like some of those grapes. And then: hang on, that's Don McGlashan, legend, fantastic songwriter, been around forever and will always remain a class act, so I shook his hand and the still life moved. I said with real feeling, 'I've always wanted to meet you.' He said, 'You have. Twice.' And then he named both occasions.

I'm as memorable as a sock but McGlashan has a mind like a steel trap, which I suppose is forever snapping at notes of music. We were both waiting to talk with host Emily Perkins about our favourite book. I asked what he'd chosen. He held up a copy of *The Periodic Table* by Primo Levi. A sudden shower of intellectual inferiority rained down on a tin roof inside my head, and drowned out what he was telling me about the book's appeal. Then I heard him ask about my book. I held up a copy of *George Best: An Intimate Biography* by Michael Parkinson. 'Look,' I said, and flipped to the title page, 'autographed!'

Fortunately, Te Radar and Wallace Chapman turned up, and I felt my intelligence returning. Thank heavens for light entertainers.

Every year I vow to cut down on public appearances. Still, a scheduled talk in May at the Auckland Literature Association ought to be a pleasant interlude, apparently I need only mutter a few words at the Auckland Writers and Readers Festival later that month, and I double-checked before agreeing to speak, briefly, at the Antarctica New Zealand annual conference in July in the knowledge that it won't be held anywhere near Antarctica.

But what the hell was I thinking when I said yes to participating in a panel discussion at the Auckland Festival of Photography in June? I bet someone will quote from Roland Barthes, that French kiss of death.

I treat media requests for my time with a strict policy: just say no. Sometimes I even follow through with it. No to appearing on the Media7 programme on digital channel 19c. No to appearing on the Summer Noelle show on Radio New Zealand ('your views on birds, celebrities, quiz culture, politics'). No, eventually, to appearing on another Radio New Zealand show, Arts on Sunday. The producers got in touch and explained they wanted me to talk about my favourite comedy tracks. Did that sound agreeable? Yes, I said. I've no idea why.

The deadline loomed, and so did a desperate excuse. I sent the programme an email: 'The truth is that I actually can't stand comedy. Never listen to it, never watch it.'

Their reply delivered unto me the sweet, dour taste of freedom.

Every few months I get a call or email from an amusing fellow who works in television. I admire him for the fact that he's written and created a funny and ingenious series – no, obviously not James Griffin, these days smearing his trademark wacky slapstick dross over every square inch of the dismal *Diplomatic Immunity*. But the amusing fellow also has his faults. Chief among them is his persistent delusion that I have something to offer. He has never quite got around to saying what. We have met only once, and talked about nothing in particular.

His latest email is bizarre, even by his standards: 'I had a good meeting at TVNZ yesterday where I discussed our series idea. There was a good response and from here they said we would need to get something on tape. So let's meet soon to work out what the show is.'

Forms arrive from the New Zealand Literary Fund. I fill them in post-haste, and send them back. The fund works out some devilishly complex equation where it measures the number of an author's books held in public libraries, divides, multiplies, rolls the dice, spins the wheel, and eventually arrives at a generous sum, which it pays out a few days before Christmas.

The form reminds me to search online library catalogues to trace the travels of my four books. They are on loan in Avondale, Remuera, Epsom, Fendalton, Riccarton, Karori, Port Chalmers, and St Andrews in Hamilton, but the best result is for two books in Blockhouse Bay, both marked: MISSING. I like the sound of that.

[April 12, 2009]

The Beginning of My Life
as a Novelist Manqué

This is a tree hut up a flight of fragile stairs. Here is the dining-room table that acts as a desk, and that is the low, soft couch where I spend most of my time. There is the view – from the front window, trees; from the back window, different trees. The soft light pads the floor in socks. This is the Frank Sargeson Centre, an upstairs studio apartment in an Auckland park, where I am writer in residence as the Buddle Findlay Sargeson Fellow.

I applied in November. I got the call in December. It did not arrive in ideal circumstances. I was cringing in a doctor's waiting room, where a very large man had burst in and begun shouting in a very loud voice. He paced from one patient to the next and prodded his finger in our sickly faces. His daughter had been beaten up; society had gone to the dogs; he had served in Vietnam and this is the thanks he got, to have his daughter set upon by bastards; New Zealand was lawless, a colony of mongrels, and no one raised a finger to stop the rot. He raised his finger. He raised his voice. He wept, he howled, he swore revenge. My phone rang. A nice woman said, 'Congratulations! You have won the Buddle Findlay Sargeson Fellowship.' I whispered, 'Thank you. Can

I call you back?'

The fellowship provides a fully furnished tree hut and a generous stipend for five months. In return, I try to make good the promise in my application. Apparently I am writing a novel. I can vouch that I am writing something. I suspect that it resembles the kind of substance that a close friend had in mind.

He's a successful novelist. I emailed him in January asking his advice. He replied, 'Here's the awful truth. You really are going to have to deal with this. Every single day is going to be a crisis of faith. Every single day.

'Except for the days you take off because you're having a crisis of faith.

'Sitting down every day and doing it is soul-destroying and gut-wrenching. For months and months and months. I don't care if you're Proust or Stephen King. People don't appreciate this. But you're all by yourself; you've got nothing to trust in except yourself. You've got nothing to show anyone at the end of the day. And what you're doing, day after day, is shit.

'Accept the first draft is going to be shit. Then revise it and make the second draft a bit better. And the third draft a bit better still. That's how books get written.'

Every one of his words rings true, and glows like burning coals. I walk over those coals every day. In bare feet. Slowly. No wonder I often feel the need for a lie-down. I sleep very well, especially in the afternoons, when I curl up on the couch. I usually dream that strangers walk in and talk with each other while I doze. It's entirely possible. I leave the front doors open. They could at least put the kettle on, or improve chapter three.

There are other voices. The park is in the grounds of Auckland University; next door is a language school, where I overhear lessons. The students are given an audio recording of a woman in a shop. She asks, 'Can I have six bananas, two apples and watermelon, please?' She is told, 'I'm sorry, but we don't have any watermelon.' I worry about the absent watermelon. Perhaps the customer is in a shoe shop. I feel like popping over and sharing my own difficulties and torments with the English language.

At night, the school's verandahs are occupied by homeless men. I am on good terms with Mark, who has introduced me to Moses. After I smoke my bedtime cigarette on the stairs, they call out across the darkness: 'Good night, Steve.' I call back: 'Good night, Mark. Good night, Moses.'

And then I head indoors and glower at the photographs of the authors who have previously held the fellowship. Their portraits are on the walls and above a bookcase. There is Janet Frame, there is Michael King, there is Bill Payne. There are also the living. Kapka Kassabova looks as though she has just heard some bad news. Paula Morris looks as though she is about to start work at *Vogue*. All of them have slept here, written here. They are the ancestors.

I've always hated ancestors. The various brilliance and

distinction of former Sargeson fellows can get too much. One afternoon I began placing the photos face down so I wouldn't have to look at them, but I quit after a couple of minutes. There were too many eyes watching.

So I bid them goodnight and fix a cup of tea, trot off to bed, and turn the light out on another day of sitting down in the earnest pursuit of destroying my soul. I pray for the morning, for another chance. The light pads in through the windows, the park fills with the sound of cicadas and parrots, chapter six waits its turn and I look around the tree hut and think: this is my very good luck, this is a state of grace.

[April 19, 2009]

Manqué Business

One month to go. The final lap, the last leg, before my term as writer in residence in an Auckland tree hut – an upstairs apartment in Auckland's Albert Park – draws to a close. I'll be sad to leave. I've enjoyed every minute of it. On a recent night of sleepless torment I wandered around the park at four a.m. and stopped outside a church where I thought I saw an autumn leaf perform an especially exquisite fall in the light of a street lamp. Closer inspection revealed it as a kingfisher. That bright, plump bird was catching moths. I watched it for about thirty minutes. And then I returned to the tree hut, where work continues slowly and unsteadily on my novel. Visitors are discouraged. But a regular guest appears each morning.

From 8.30 sharp until the exact stroke of 9.15, an ugly Korean man performs t'ai chi right outside the apartment. I want to roar at him in plain English: 'Clear off!' But a park is a public place, there for all to act the fool. He switches on a cheap transistor. It plays what might be described as music. Flutes and other instruments of torture rise up and wail through my window. I hate the ugly Korean. I hate his awful music. I hate his stupid exercises, which reach a climax when he swipes the air with a fold-up plastic sword. Sometimes I stand at the top of the stairs and glower at him. He glowers back. Behold the dysfunctional relationship of the novelist manqué and the t'ai chi master.

The rest of the morning is quiet, solitary. I sit at a long table and reach out for cups of tea and chocolate biscuits. Less frequently, my paws fumble at the keyboard. There are times when I think the best thing about winning the Buddle Findlay Sargeson Fellowship was winning the Buddle Findlay Sargeson Fellowship. That was a good moment. The actual work is a tide of misery, agony, despair and self-loathing. Mostly, though, I think about what I'm doing and what I'm trying to do. Time passes. There are none of the usual distractions. I deliberately have no email or internet access. But now and then the afternoon is interrupted by goings-on at the language school next door.

The latest episode occurred when I heard a commotion outside the back window. About a dozen students were running from tree to tree. I drew up a chair, and resumed spying. The trees were decorated with strips of paper. One tree was marked ADJECTIVE, another tree NOUN, and so on. The teacher called out words; the students had to run to the correct tree. There was a lot of laughter. At first I admired the lesson, and thought: that's an ingenious teaching idea. But then I realised I was also witnessing a cruel parody of my own struggles with English. The fumbling at the keyboard, the pursuit of language: writing a novel can feel like you're lost in a dark forest. You can't see the wood for the trees. Sometimes you can't see the trees... I drew the curtain, and returned to the couch for a lie-down.

It's a really good couch. It welcomes my notion that an afternoon nap really ought to last all afternoon. I'm usually back on my feet by about four p.m., when I fix a snack and then fix the morning's work. Autumn twilight is beautiful in the park. The trees soften, the wind dies. Gentle rain often falls just as dusk falls. The city towers disappear. It's a nice time for a stroll: Princes Street, with its plane trees and its ginkgo trees, its stone walls and its shapely clock tower, may be the loveliest street in Auckland. I think how lucky I am to spend my time writing in a serene apartment in that end of town, and then I trot back up the stairs to paw at the next chapter. The nights are silent, undisturbed. An unplugged TV gathers dust in a corner. But sometimes I walk into the evening to attend literary events.

A past winner of the fellowship recently launched her new book. She attracted a large crowd. It included other writers, as well as academics, a painter, an actress, a shifty-looking QC. Some fop made a boring speech, and then the author gave a very good speech. She mentioned a dream she had while writing her book. A monk in a black cape appeared and said something about flowers – I didn't quite catch the drift, but the point of the dream was that it acted as a meta-phor for how she should structure her book.

Something deep in my subconscious was obviously

inspired. I had a vivid dream later that night, and it didn't take me long to see it as a metaphor. It illustrated the experience of writing my book. I dreamed that I was stumbling around a dark room, got my foot stuck in the bars of an electric heater, and my foot started to smoke...

I woke up whimpering in imagined pain. I couldn't get back to sleep. I wandered around the park, and found myself staring at a bright, plump kingfisher under a streetlight at four a.m.

[May 24, 2009]

The End of My Life as
a Novelist Manqué

Farewell, then, the Fellowship. My tenure as writer in residence is over, gone, past its use-by date. I hoofed it yesterday, cradling a cardboard box of personal effects — laptop, biscuits — on my last walk down the stairs, leading away from those rooms touched with soft light, away from Albert Park, away from the ginkgo trees and the grapefruit trees and the escaped parrots in the gum trees.

I was there for five months. I began writing a novel. Apart from confronting the dark three a.m. of the soul at any time of day, when the book was going badly and I'd idly wonder just how many bones I could break in my body if I jumped out the window, I adored every second of it. The trees, the birds, the light. It was so quiet. I once enjoyed the pleasure of a term at Oxford, but the Frank Sargeson Centre actually did feel like a dreaming spire.

It was a tree hut. Its one small front window was made smaller by the ivy that scratched at the glass. I would sit there, my little face peering out at the big city beyond the tops of the trees, at the homeless men who slept on the verandah of the language school next door. 'Frank's kind of people,' wrote Janet Frame, the first writer to be awarded the fellowship, in 1987. I thought often about Sargeson, about his resilience, his generosity of spirit. One warm afternoon I was sitting on the front steps when a homeless guy appeared with a six-pack of Cody's bourbon and coke under his arm. He said, 'Can I come up?' I said, 'No, you can't.' He said, 'Why not? We're neighbours.'

I was the pampered hermit on a stipend, solitary inside an ivy tower. Worse, I found myself reduced to playing that stock character of low farce, the wild-haired eccentric. I would pace the floor, upturning cushions and scattering papers in a search for my reading glasses, and finally realise they were on my head. Another homeless guy said one morning, 'Are you a professor?' 'No,' I said, and then he fell over.

He lay beside a park bench for about ten minutes. There had been a lot of dew. The grass was as thick as a sponge. He seemed oblivious to his discomfort. I was sensitive to the slightest twinge of my own exquisite pain. Hermit, eccentric, professor – I could suffer those clichés, but I feared the possibility I was playing at being a novelist. Any resemblance may have been only superficial. Was it all just on loan? The keys to the tree hut have been returned, and I must get around to giving the laptop back to Wellington writer Neil Cross. His friendship was entirely crucial. I would phone the poor devil and whine in his ear, especially around the time I knew I'd made a false start on the book. I collapsed on the couch for two, maybe three weeks. So little time to write my first novel; so much of it wasted.

But I made an important discovery. Crawling across the floor one day to the bookshelf, I found two very long novels by modern New Zealand writers. Both books were so rotten, so phoney and boring, so insanely praised. ... I put on the kettle and wrote the first seven chapters.

A table, a couch, a kettle. It was spartan living. I made it more spartan. I closed off the bedroom, and made up a stretcher bed beside my writing table in the kitchen. I took all the paintings off the walls and stowed them in a dark cupboard. The framed photographs of previous fellows were next to go: I placed them face-down on the bookshelf. I hated their excellence, their confident fizzogs. Their absence left nothing to look at. I liked that.

When I arrived, I wrote up an inventory of stock. Oven mitts, lens cleaning tissues, a 2008 calendar from Lotsa Shoes in Onehunga Mall, a can of sardines, a candle... It barely filled half a page. Good. The place was crammed with something else – patience, silence. It was a garret, but I never starved. When I arrived I laid in supplies, which consisted mainly of lots of packets of biscuits.

I loved my life on a mezzanine floor. There was a skylight, and it had a high ceiling – historically, it was a horse stables. I thought sometimes about the nineteenth-century merchants of Princes Street walking over to feed their mares a turnip. The same place now hosted a biscuit-nibbling jackass, but I was house-proud, kept a tidy ship, and dumped paper and plastics into the recycling bin next door. There was a bin under the stairs, but the homeless men used that for their bedding. One of them said, 'I thought, Steve won't mind. You don't, do you?' I said, 'Why would I? We're neighbours.'

Ex-neighbours. The fellowship was the best thing that's ever happened to me in my writing life but I wanted to go home. I was the absent father, the estranged fiancé. I wrote half the book. I'll finish it under my own roof. It should take only another five, maybe six months, or longer. I took something away from the tree hut: the simple lesson of resilience.

[July 5, 2009]

Grub Street: On Tour

To Whanganui, that beautiful, fragile oasis of water and cherry blossom, for the city's literary festival. I meet Auckland food writer Ray McVinnie, who opens the weekend festival when he appears onstage with Alexa Johnston, the funny and charming author of a modern masterpiece, *Ladies, A Plate: Traditional Home Baking*.

Together, the sweet powdery scent of their celebrity entices a big crowd. How big? My eyes fall on a sheet of paper listing pre-booked sales for each event. Nervously, with a black heart, I look to find the three most popular attractions. Third, on fifty-seven tickets, Dame Fiona Kidman. Second, on sixty-three, Ray and Alexa. I am in front by a nose on sixty-four. Good.

Door sales just about double the attendance at every show. Book sales, too, are brisk. A local bookstore sets up a table at the festival venue. 'We've just about sold out our stock of your books,' says the nice woman from Poppies Books. Good. 'So,' she adds, 'I desperately phoned up Whitcoulls and Paper Plus to order more.' Good. But then she says, 'They didn't have any. They'd never even heard of you. What they said was, "Steve who?"'

A chance encounter with one of New Zealand's most distinguished novelists at a fish and chip shop. Anxious and fretful, he sits hunched over a manuscript, writing and crossing out in neat longhand. 'I'm on deadline,' he says. I wish him luck. And then his order is announced: one scoop of chips, one sausage. Strange to consider the role of the sausage in New Zealand literature. When my friend at the fish and chip shop has his book published, I will think back to that evening when he slaved away at his manuscript, fought hard for each word, kept pace with the marathon effort of completing a novel, and found sustenance, possibly even inspiration, in that single solitary sausage.

My application for a writer's award proves unsuccessful. Bother. I thought I had arrived at an excellent idea for a biography of a New Zealand historical figure. Perhaps the working title was too negative: *In the Name of the Wretch*.

Haruki Murakami, the great Japanese writer, recently wrote a kind of inner monologue called *What I Talk About When I Talk About Running*. He competes in marathons. It occupies a lot of his time and thinking. I can relate to that: I mow lawns – my lawn and the lawn of a frail neighbour. It's a test of physical and mental endurance. I take it very seriously, keep focussed, maintain straight, elegant lines, attend to difficult edges. All the while – forty-five minutes for my lawn, an hour for hers – my mind twirls like a twin blade. My application for the next annual writers' awards will detail the proposal for a book called *What I Talk About When I Talk About Mowing*.

Apparently a new television series inspired by my book *How to Watch a Bird* went to air last night. I worked on the show as a kind of consultant. The producers sent unfinished tapes of each episode. I suggested various script amendments. Later they sent the finished tapes. I watched a couple. There was only one word I knew I'd written – the title, *Birdland*.

To damp Titirangi for the Going West literary festival, where I conduct an onstage interview with Keith Woodley, author of the superb new book *Godwits: Long-haul Champions*. I like playing support act. All I have to do is sit back, listen, and now and then prod Keith with a question. He does the rest, and dazzles a full house with his droll wit, easy manner and enthusiastic knowledge.

Once again I give thought to my notion of leading a nationwide, week-long stage tour of authors. No sleep until Timaru, etc. I approach a government agency. Its chief executive replies, 'I really like the idea and definitely think it would work.' All it needs is sponsorship. And authors. I draw up a list of New Zealand writers who have stage presence. It's a very long list. Then I think about who would still talk to each other by the end of the tour. It's a fairly long list. Then I think about who would still talk to me by the end of the tour.

Never mind.

My first book, published eight long years ago, continues to attract new readers, still does the business; strange to reflect on the endurance of *Fool's Paradise*, its literary staying power, its unique and unshakable place in the hearts of New Zealanders, as a royalty cheque arrives from Random House for $40.17.

That's a lot of sausages.

[October 4, 2009]

Yes, V.S.

Gore Vidal wrote of V.S. Pritchett in 1979: 'It would be nice if he lived forever.' The old boy came close. Pritchett was born 1900, died 1997 – almost the whole of that century at his fingertips, transcribing its comedy and violence, its unglamorous working life and brittle domestic affairs in over a hundred short stories, various travel writings, and two volumes of autobiography. He became incapable of writing a bad sentence. He was famous in his time – knighted, revered. But who reads him anymore? Who even knows the name?

I came to Pritchett only recently. Now and then I draw up a comfortable chair in an empty room next to my office and dip into a bookcase. I reached in last month and took out Pritchett's memoir *Midnight Oil*. It had been lent to me by Auckland poet Bob Orr about two or three years ago. Bob has the finest reading taste of any writer I know. His recommendations have included Mikhail Bulgakov, Laurie Lee, and one of the very best authors of cowboy novels, Glendon Swarthout. I don't know why it took me so long to read his Pritchett. The title was merely unfortunate: I couldn't blame Pritchett for it sharing the name of a foul Australian rawk band. His stuffy initials, though, and the cover photograph of an ancient Pritchett sitting bent-backed at his writing desk – I suppose the book stank of old literature.

But it was a revelation. Reading *Midnight Oil* with immediate awe, and then racing off, intoxicated, to his fiction and essays, is to be confronted with someone who observed life with such nuance, wit, affection and easy intelligence that every page is fresh. In his short stories, his characters work for a living – shopkeepers, window cleaners, salesmen, barmaids. Pritchett was lower middle class. He left England as a young man and found a job with a glue manufacturer in Paris. He writes in *Midnight Oil*: 'When I read memoirs about the Paris of Joyce, Hemingway and Fitzgerald, I am cast down. I was there. I may have seen them in the street; I had simply never heard of them. ... I did not know that I was living in the centre of a literary revolution. I was an outsider.'

Later, he conferenced with Nabokov, dined with Greene, was on the inside with the good and the mad. Pritchett on Cyril Connolly: 'I often thought of him in middle age as a phenomenal baby in a pram.' And on Wyndham Lewis: 'He sat like a flaccid, deaf and expiring tortoise on a sofa.' He was on a retainer with *The New Yorker* – the magazine had first option on his stories – and admired as the most fluent literary critic since Edmund Wilson.

Pritchett may well have been the most bookish man of the twentieth century. Too poor for university, he educated himself in the classics, read and devoured and shared; his literary essays owe nothing to boring academic discourse stuffed with jargon and French intellectual merde. On *Huckleberry Finn*: 'Out of the mess which Mark Twain made of his life, amid the awful pile of tripe which he wrote, there does rise one book which has the serenity of a thing of genius.' In that same essay, his epigrammatic prose style has him describe Twain and Edgar Allan Poe as 'that pair of spiritual derelicts, those two scarecrow figures with their half-lynched minds'.

The critic Clifton Fadiman heads a list of Pritchett's distinguishing qualities as a writer with this virtue: 'Sanity'. Pritchett always kept a clear head. He knew his own mind, and developed a genius to inhabit the minds of others – the antique dealers and their dusty wives in his story 'The Camberwell Beauty', the hapless, sodden accountant in 'The Fall'. Martin Amis, an admirer of Pritchett, describes the short stories as 'feminine'. I think that's a comment on their delicacy, their lack of the author's ego. Pritchett never bursts in on a story with a windy literary entrance.

Wise, modest, sane – it makes him a hard sell beyond the grave. Worse, there's no scandal, no advertisement for his failings. His sympathetic biographer, Jeremy Treglown, reveals an alcoholic wife, a tortured affair with some American broad. But his subject fails as a figure of tabloid interest. It's a portrait of a resolutely nice man who worked hard, nursed a tumbler at his club, suffered from gout, was moved into a nursing home and mistook a grandson for his bank manager. Nothing to see here. Move on.

You're left with what matters: the writing. There are the subtle techniques, the musical patterns — Amis has typically acute things to say about Pritchett's masterly use of the comma. He's probably doomed to be viewed, or half-remembered, as a writer's writer. It's a false charge. He was a reader's writer. He began his trade as a kind of journalist, working as a correspondent in Ireland, Paris and Spain, writing rather self-conscious sketches. But he appreciated the demands of an audience. As a short story writer, he was loyal to his characters. Pritchett, the old pro; Pritchett, attentive and meticulous, laughing and tender, his imagination able to phrase something as amazing as 'half-lynched minds'; Pritchett, in essence, the living writer.

[October 18, 2009]

A Year on Grub Street

So, 2009: one literary fellowship, half a novel. I never had it so good as those five woozy, luxurious months of solitude and rare privilege as writer in residence in an Albert Park tree hut. I ate so many biscuits. Milk Arrowroot, Krispies – a packet a day, the happy satisfying crunch of their steadily declining contents the only sound to be heard in those lovely quiet rooms up the stairs. When it came time to depart, I left with crumbs: half a novel, half-empty.

But I arrived with nothing. Only a rough and ambitious idea, which began to find its way on to paper. It was the hardest thing I ever attempted to write and the best thing I ever wrote. It put one foot in front of another. Slowly, carefully. It moved like an old man.

The only direction it's taken these past few months is backwards – rewriting earlier chapters, taking out the trash. Well, it had to be done. The book is better for it. Half a novel, halfway there. But how to move forward?

Recent events in New Zealand publishing suggest a post-modern solution: plagiarise *The Trowenna Sea*, the new novel by Witi Ihimaera. He's not exactly in any position to complain since *Public Address* blogger and *Listener* reviewer

Jolisa Gracewood collared him for plagiarising about twenty passages from other books. Plus, I like Witi: he's a good and decent fellow. It might take the heat off him if I got in on the act by re-plagiarising those same passages, then raised the stakes by plagiarising whole chapters from *The Trowenna Sea*. My novel would be finished quick sharp.

The worst that could happen is that, like Witi, I will receive a $50,000 Arts Laureate award.

The television series inspired by a book I wrote two years ago apparently rated very well. That's nice. And it was a pleasant feeling to generate the spending of public money: New Zealand On Air forked out $433,855 to *Birdland*. I got an okay fee. A shame, though, that producer Phil Smith didn't bother replying to any of the correspondence sent by my publisher, who thought it might be good manners to include some mention of the book in the show's credits.

Never mind. That's television. But the book has enjoyed a second life on radio. Emails from a man in Invercargill and a woman in Katikati earlier this month alerted me to the news that Radio New Zealand replayed the reading I gave of *How to Watch a Bird*. The original broadcast was played in daily instalments over a week on the Nine to Noon show. The latest broadcast was played in nightly instalments over a week on the All Night programme.

I have always wanted to stake my claim to the dark 3.15 a.m of the New Zealand soul.

One catalogue for an exhibition at the Christchurch Art Gallery. Two broadcasting jobs: the reluctant decision to say yes to appearing as a regular guest bore on Radio New Zealand; another reluctant decision to say yes to appearing as a regular guest bore on a television show. Three weekly columns: this one and a satire in *The Sunday Star-Times*; another satire syndicated to four newspapers. Four publishers wanting my unfinished novel, five travel assignments as a journalist – I survived Antarctica, also Mosgiel.

Working across different media really is known in the trade as 'creating a portfolio'. Engaging in so many fields really is known in the trade as 'establishing a brand', and 'building a profile'.

I really must get around to lining myself up against a wall to be shot.

It gets worse. One, two, three ... nineteen public appearances. Talks, lectures, speeches, that sort of thing, as well as a televised literary debate in an Auckland church. I watched the show when it went to air. When it came to my turn, I fled the house, and stood in the dark outside the living room, peering through the blinds at my fiancée watching me on TV. I watched her laughing. I felt enormous waves of love and gratitude. I also felt terribly afraid that some Neighbourhood Watch busybody was about to call the cops.

The appearance I enjoyed most was talking about birds as guest speaker at the Ornithological Society of New Zealand's annual conference in Orewa. It was held at the same venue where poor old Don Brash made his infamous speech about another kind of native species.

The appearances I hated most were at Otago University, where I gave a lame and incoherent speech in the evening, and an even more ridiculous address the next day when I took part in a symposium about the media's role in reporting global warming. I had no right to be there. I don't report global warming. I go out of my way to avoid reading about global warming. It was strange to talk in those two rooms in Dunedin, and feel the air freeze.

New Year's resolution: no public appearances in 2010. I'm busy. I've a novel to complete. Its working title is *The Trowenna Sea*.

[November 29, 2009]

Correspondence

Yes, time again for the annual trawl through letters and emails sent in by readers. Pasted into a file, this year's emails weighed in at 39,975 words, up by about four thousand from last year, and up in mood, too. 'Dickens would have loved it,' wrote Jeffrey of Christchurch, responding to a column about Fairlie. 'It brought to mind Joyce and Camus,' emailed Alex, responding to a column about Point Chevalier. I began to miss receiving hate mail. Hate mail duly arrived. By post, Angeline wrote: 'Your malicious columns ... tabloid ... tatty ... slanderous. ... Shame on you and your type.' Did she mean Dickens, Joyce, Camus? Angeline signed off by admitting: 'I'm American.'

'Thanks for the best read, week after week,' Alan emailed, 'in the *Listener*.' No problem, although I don't write for the *Listener*. Robyn of Nelson, in January: 'You should have received a New Year's Honour.' Jean of Otaki had other ideas regarding official recognition. Made mentally unstable by a loving column about my infant daughter, she wrote: 'It should be made compulsory to hand it out to every new parent when a baby is registered.' But the same column set off a hostile email exchange with Ann. She dared to condemn my parenting. I replied, huffily: 'What a stupid and offensive little email.' She replied, stuffily: 'You are typical of today's younger generation.' Younger generation! That was nice of the old bag.

A friendlier exchange came after a column about the death of that spectacular wretch, the murderer and butcher Antonie Dixon. 'I thought of all the media output about him yours came closest to getting it right,' emailed Justin of Wellington. He is a forensic psychiatrist. He had assessed Dixon. I asked him whether he agreed that his former client was, in fact, someone who just wasn't very interesting. He replied: 'To be honest I haven't met many people like Mr Dixon.' Another way of putting it came from an anonymous reader who claimed to have met 'Mr Dixon' a few years ago. 'He went out to play with a pit bull by swinging a T-shirt around for it to catch. It was then realised that the T-shirt was a cat.'

Crime writing always appeals. Geography separated Christine of Remuera from Freda of Gore, but both had witnessed, and suffered, the same lack of human decency I revealed in a column about the monstrous selfishness of neighbours who mow only their half of the shared grass verge on the pavement.

An offer of work came from Heather: 'We are currently producing a 3D animated comedy series. Is this something you might like to get involved with?' Interesting. But then she shared a vision of bland hell: 'We have recorded the first episode with Oliver Driver, Ewen Gilmour and Jono Pryor.'

I also heard from a professor of endocrinology, an expert in the life cycle of the Adélie penguin, the CEO of a sauce factory, and Gwen, 80, of Rotorua, who once knew a family of criminals in Sydney. 'One got murdered and two got stabbed in the throat and left to die but were rescued. You can see that Rotorua is a bit quiet for me.'

Addresses from other readers included Ngunguru, Lumsden, Orakei, Greytown, Glenfield, Te Kopuru, Riverton, Motueka, Bluff, Sydenham, Trentham, Hamilton East, Cromwell, even remote Karori. 'Thank you for your columns,' emailed Kelvin. 'They regularly move me because they express a New Zealand I want to believe in.'

But I am regularly moved by readers who express a New Zealand I can scarcely imagine. A column about unemployment had Lenny of Tokoroa describe attending meaningless job seminars at WINZ, 'sitting behind a Mob member in a room full of Black Power supporters.' He now runs a community gallery providing out-of-school services for local kids and is 'doing a business plan based on converting pickup trucks to plug-in electric vehicles.'

A column about the sentencing of Clayton Weatherston had Lesley of Dunedin reply, 'We are so sad that our daughter at twenty-two did not have life's experiences to recognise him for what he is.' Like Sophie Elliott's mother's conduct in public, her email was a miracle of grace.

An email from Ron of Mairangi Bay was something else: 'I am about to hand you a story that is on a par with the Arthur Allen Thomas case.' It had something to do with the Bain murders. At the end of his 1305-word email, Ron wrote: 'I have developed a whole lot more and sundry other stuff but I am getting tired. If you wish to pursue this further give me a ring.' I was too tired. Besides, we already know who killed the Bains.

Practical assistance came from Martin. Responding to a column about feeding garden birds, he wrote, 'Buy a 375-gram jar of smooth peanut butter made in China (it tastes awful) from New World. I put my jar into a tangle of clematis about two metres from the kitchen window. It takes the silvereye flock about a week to empty the pot. I like to watch them while making the evening sandwiches.' He was right. It tastes awful. But the jar transformed my backyard into a happy mania of silvereyes. They were as small, active and welcome as 39,975 words.

[December 13, 2009]

Dad's Book

Behold the New Zealand dad, in summer, on holiday, relaxing with his book. He might be at the seaside with his book. He might be in a caravan with his book. He might just be at home, happy to slop around, light the barbecue, uncork another bottle, and sit in the shade with his book.

What's he reading? Dad doesn't want literature. He's tired, for God's sake; give him a break. And he's not in the mood right now to learn about managing his finances from Gareth Morgan, or read the apparently amazing life story of Michael Hill Jeweller. He wants a good fat fast-paced thriller. He wants stuff blown up. He wants men of action – men like himself, really, if the truth be known. He wants Jack Reacher.

Reacher, ex-army, a maverick of no fixed abode, blue-eyed, with fists 'the size of footballs'; Reacher, the hero of thirteen novels by the world's biggest-selling action writer, Lee Child. The latest is *Gone Tomorrow*, but the great thing about Reacher books is that you can read them in any order you choose. New Zealand dad opens up *Die Trying*, published in 1998. He can tell straight off the bat that it's a thumping good read. It says on the inside cover that it won the WH

Smith Thumping Good Read Award.

He adjusts the sun umbrella. It's a beautiful summer's day. And it's hot in Chicago, too. Chapter one: 'Centre of the city, a busy sidewalk, a Monday, last day of June. Broad daylight, bright summer sunshine. The whole situation had materialised in a split second.' Yes, because there's Reacher minding his own business, politely opening the door for a woman who has her hands full with her dry-cleaning, when suddenly four guys armed with a 9mm Glock 17 hustle the two of them into the back of a waiting car.

Reacher doesn't go looking for trouble. It comes looking for him. The thing to do is keep cool. Assess the situation. Calculate the odds. Above all, shrug. 'He shrugged at her. ... He looked at her and shrugged. ... He moved a half-inch closer and shrugged. ... She asked, "Who are you?" He smiled and shrugged.' But soon enough he's ripping off someone's head with his bare, football-sized hands.

Excellent, thinks New Zealand dad, then puts the book down – the family are clamouring for a picnic lunch. He helps pack up the car, pockets the keys to the rented cottage, and drives to a nearby beach. They carry baskets and bottles down a steep track of native forest; it opens out on to a secluded bay. The water is lovely. Wonderful to swim, eat kai, read Reacher, doze, and then it's time to leave. But wait! Where are the keys to the cottage? Oh, Christ. He gets on his hands and knees and brushes the sand. Nothing! Oh, God. What to do? You can't break into the cottage – glass everywhere, the owners would have a fit. The holiday is ruined. The family bicker and puff their way up the track to the car. Look in the glove box – you never know. Haw! There's the keys! Good old dad! Add that one to the family's secret history.

Reacher and the woman, FBI special agent Holly Johnson, have been kidnapped by a cult. The cult leader, Borken, wants to wage war. 'Holly asked, "Suppose they're working for Iraq?" Reacher shrugged. She asked, "So what the hell is this about?" Reacher shrugged again.' And again and again, but he's got stiff competition. 'The sheriff shrugged ... Borken shrugged ... Holly shrugged across the distance at him.' Reacher raises the stakes: 'He shrugged as he walked.' Meanwhile, an innocent passer-by is shredded with a chainsaw, and stuff blows up.

As the afternoon cools New Zealand dad hoses the garden. He switches the nozzle, which he bought at Hammer Hardware for $6.99, to jet. The radishes are looking good, there are still a few strawberries, the beans are standing tall. He switches the nozzle to shower.

Reacher reaches for a weapon: the Baretta. 'It delivered quarter-ounce bullets at nearly 800 miles an hour.' Holly watches his heroics with hot interest. 'They kissed. She felt lithe and athletic. Firm, but soft. Young. Scented...'

New Zealand mum says, 'We've run out of bread and sauce.' Dad drives to the town's only store. Two longhaired girls are outside licking ice creams, their knees drawn up as they sit on the bonnet of their car. Their skin is so smooth in the summer twilight. They don't look at him.

Later that night, New Zealand dad grunts as he sits down on his canvas chair outside the caravan to finish his book. Goddamned mosquitoes! He slaps on the Dimp. Reacher kills everyone who needs killing. 'The bullet entered the front of Borken's forehead and was out of the back of his skull three ten-thousandths of a second later. ... It travelled over the forest before the pressure wave built up in Borken's skull and exploded it.'

The end. Reacher has somewhere else to go: 'Longest I've stayed anywhere was ten consecutive days.' New Zealand dad has somewhere else to go: work. One last night of precious holiday, then back to the daily grind. Oh well. Dad stretches, yawns, and then – manfully, powerfully, a quiet hero of real life – shrugs.

[January 24, 2010]

A Brief History of New Zealand Literature

Everybody who is anybody in New Zealand letters appeared at the New Zealand Post Writers and Readers Week in Wellington earlier this month, apart from Maurice Gee, Witi Ihimaera, C.K. Stead, Stephanie Johnson, Brian Turner, Eleanor Catton, Patricia Grace, David Hill, Keri Hulme, Alan Duff, Anthony McCarten, Sam Hunt, Margaret Mahy, Tom Scott, Chad Taylor, Kapka Kassabova, Owen Marshall and a few hundred others, but everybody else was there. Emily Perkins was there with her brood. Dame Fiona Kidman was there with her brooch. And so the grand old Embassy Theatre in Kent Terrace, saved and restored by a Trust that included Sir Peter Jackson, became a kind of literary ghetto for a week – in the lobbies, the women came and went, talking of Albert Wendt.

The authors from out of town were put up in the Copthorne on Oriental Bay. I checked in on Thursday morning and met London novelist Geoff Dyer. Let's hook up later, I said. Good, he said, I'll text you my number. And then I sat in my room to memorise the introduction and questions for poet Bill Manhire, whom I was chairing that afternoon. He gave a marvellous fluid performance to an audience of maybe two hundred, three hundred. Afterwards, he signed books for a long queue of well-dressed old dears. I think I saw former Labour MP Judith Tizard. I think I spoke with current Labour MP Steve Chadwick. As a government minister, she tried to ban smoking in the southern hemisphere. She – Chadwick, or a woman who looked like Chadwick – scowled and said, 'I was in the audience. You were very ... controlling.' I ran outside for a cigarette.

I definitely spoke with Glen Rowling, who was married to former Labour prime minister Bill Rowling. She smiled, and said, 'That was the best chairing I've ever seen at the festival.' I thought: your husband was one of the most decent politicians in New Zealand's history. But I also thought: hang on, is he dead or alive? And then a nice man with grey hair arrived at her side. I grabbed his hand for dear life and roared: 'It's a great pleasure to meet you!' Later, I realised it probably wasn't Bill Rowling because he died in 1995.

I was stone lukewarm sober. By six p.m., at the nearby launch for three books of poetry published by Victoria University Press, I was blind drunk, but still able to make out a Hollywood celebrity. I sidled up to novelist Rachael King. 'I have something important to tell you,' I said. 'The man sitting behind you is actor John Goodman.' She turned and said, 'It's the economist Brian Easton.' I remarked on their incredible resemblance to novelist Damien Wilkins, who asked about the progress of my novel, and whether I'd spoken with a publisher. I mentioned a publisher. He pointed to a serviette on the floor. It was smeared with olive oil and sundried tomato. He said, 'They'd publish that.' I said, 'Have you just insulted me?' He said, 'You insulted my wife.' I said, 'Did I?'

And then I ran into musician Alan Janssen, who produced 'How Bizarre' by Pauly Fuemana and 'Pulsing' by The Body Electric, and we left to drive around the Wellington bays for an hour in the rain. It was just like old times, except he drove a hybrid car, and he pointed out a rambling structure that seemed to curl around and hog an entire promontory – the sea cowered beneath it. He said, 'Peter Jackson's house.' It looked haunted, mad, big enough for both John Goodman and Brian Easton. Back in town I checked my phone. A text read: 'Can u call me in rm 1015.' I thought: oho! But it was only Geoff Dyer, and he couldn't come out. I arranged to meet novelist Neil Cross. We were getting on splendidly, but then he said, 'I'm going home. You've been insulting me ever since you arrived.' I said, 'Have I?' Somehow or other I salvaged our friendship, and I collapsed at the Copthorne at two or five in the morning.

After I woke up, I sat in my room to memorise the introduction and questions for novelist Charlotte Grimshaw, whom I was chairing in the afternoon. I worked on that for a while, then phoned her up. She was in the next room. She said she'd slept with the sliding doors open, and received great gusts of smoke billowing from a neighbouring balcony at two or five in the morning. Tut-tut, I said. Her 2.15 p.m.

session went very well: to an audience of maybe 300, 400, she read a fascinating passage about a National Party leader on the campaign trail. It was an excerpt from her new novel. No, she said, the politician wasn't based on John Key. Her character had an inner life.

Afterwards, in the Embassy lounge, a festival manager said, 'Would you like a drink?' I said, 'Yes, please.' I nursed the whisky for a slow hour. Chairing authors is exhausting work. So is Wellington, with its weird storms, its bubbling drains, its cottages on the edge of cliff and water, its sensitive feelings, its quality talk. I returned to dumb, blasé Auckland, to that unpublished serviette in progress.

[March 28, 2010]

Dear Patricia

Last year it was *This Sweet Sickness*, late at night, as writer in residence in an upstairs loft in Auckland's Albert Park. This year it's *The Blunderer*, on the Overlander train every Tuesday morning and again in the early evening, when I commute between Auckland and Hamilton as editor in residence at Wintec. I don't know where I'll be next year, but I'll definitely reread another novel by Patricia Highsmith.

Rereading a genius is one of literature's greatest pleasures. You think you'll know what to expect – you went this way before, you can retrace your steps. It's the same words. Your hands held the same pages. But genius always takes you somewhere else. You don't know where you are. You're completely lost. You've gone somewhere even better than you first imagined.

Patricia Highsmith always does that. She set most of her weird art in anonymous American suburbs. She wrote suspense novels, thrillers – a paperback writer. She liked the commercial form; rugged up inside it, she got on with her vocation of torment. She tormented her characters, put them on the ledge and then pushed. Her books can read like nihilistic fantasies. 'We are suffering from nihilism,' said

Albert Camus, one of Highsmith's favourite authors. Camus was mirthless. Highsmith enjoyed her nihilism.

She was heartily un-American. Born in Fort Worth, Texas, in 1921, died at seventy-four in Locarno, Switzerland, where she chose to live in exile. A voracious lesbian, she reserved a special hatred in her books for women. Unfaithful, venal, dumb, clinging, worthless – her characters are a parade of stupid bitches, and a great many of them end up murdered. As a misogynist Highsmith was astounding. It gave her so much happiness. There's a smile working its way through the pages; you could read her books in the dark by the light shining in her amused, tormenting eyes.

Poor, sweet, dim Effie Brennan in *This Sweet Sickness*: 'She had large, square front teeth.' We don't ever see much more of her than that, and never see inside her mind. All the attention is lavished on David Kelsey, who is almost totally insane. 'It was the last straw, this common little stenographer crashing into his house, telling him that she loved him. ... David moved toward her. She groped for the doorknob, still staring at him with her terrified eyes, as if he had just beaten her within an inch of her life.' After he crosses that inch, he dines out in a New York restaurant with Annabelle, the woman of his dreams. I reread that scene over and over late one night in Albert Park, amazed at Highsmith's inventive black comedy – the intimate dinner, the two orders of clams and veal. 'He poured two glasses of wine when the meat dish arrived, and the more the waiters looked at him, the more nonchalantly he chatted with Annabelle.' But Annabelle isn't there. David Kelsey is by now totally insane.

Highsmith's classic madman, Tom Ripley, featured in five of her books, and was delicately played by Matt Damon in the film version of *The Talented Mr Ripley*. The suspense in her Ripley books was how the madman would get away with murder – Highsmith estimates eight victims – and the charm of it all was the absolute moral vacuum. No punishment, no justice: those themes likely appealed to her admirer and occasional correspondent Graham Greene, another genius of fiction and hate.

Actually, Highsmith sometimes wrote very tenderly about love. But she was fascinated with disorder and collapse; slowly, patiently, coldly, she probed the human mind for every sign of distress. Reviewers meant it as a compliment when they called her work 'inhuman'. Highsmith, according to an enemy: 'Relentlessly ugly.' According to a friend: 'Very difficult.'

Like the wretched cuckold Victor Van Allen in her novel *Deep Water*, she bred snails. She was an alcoholic. She was accused of anti-Semitism, which is always an easy insult. Her novel *People Who Knock on the Door* is dedicated 'to the courage of the Palestinian people and their leaders in the struggle to regain a part of their homeland'. She adds: 'This book has nothing to do with their problem.' It has a lot to do with her loathing of evangelical Christianity. Does a woman get killed? Probably, although I cannot remember. I may reread it next year, but I think I'll choose either *The Glass Cell*, about a morphine addict who suspects his wife is having an affair, or Highsmith's acknowledged masterpiece *The Cry of the Owl*, about a woman who falls in love with her stalker.

Poor, sweet, dim Ellie Briess — strange that she shares the same initials as the victim in *This Sweet Sickness* — falls in love with the wrong man in *The Blunderer*. He entertains thoughts about committing a copycat murder. His worst crime, though, is that he's a hapless individual. It's awful and hilarious to watch Highsmith make him squirm as Tuesday's train rattles back and forth beside the Waikato River. A cup of tea from the buffet car, a death; the view of crops and swamp, the anatomy of disorder and collapse... It only occurs to me now that I should have chosen to reread her first novel. Albert Hitchcock made it famous when he directed *Strangers On A Train*.

[May 2, 2010]

The Train to Hamilton

It was all about rhythm. It was the rhythm of Tuesdays, when I rolled out of bed at six a.m. and quietly left the sleeping house to commute to Hamilton, where I work one day a week. It was the rhythm of the Overlander, its sharp whistles and low hoots, its smooth diesel engine, its compact metal hulk clattering on the tracks. It left Auckland at seven-thirty a.m. and returned from Hamilton at about five p.m. I rode it six times in late summer into autumn. The service has now reverted to its winter timetable and runs only on Friday, Saturday and Sunday, until September. For the next few months, my commute is by bus. Not the same? It's nothing like it.

I loved every second as a commuter on the two hours and twenty minutes' journey through three zones: cramped South Auckland, Franklin county with its crops and hawks, the damp Waikato plains. I loved looking at things, I loved reading, I loved falling asleep – the clatter fell to a hush, like the whispering in a library. I loved the boring seconds. A train is a vacuum. Nothing happens; it's passive, dreamy, private. And I loved stepping outside on to the viewing platform – a thin, shuddering floor between two carriages, open to wind and rain, to the scent of river and soil. Summer turned to autumn, the light faded; I always took my seat in the buffet car, in the soft red seats designed by Lazzarini; I faded on every journey, and dozed.

But I hated missing the sight of the river, the broad Waikato, its surge as quiet but more powerful than the train. Travelling south, it showed itself at Mercer, and it did something to the landscape – opened it out, and somehow relaxed it. Taupiri and Ngaruawahia hung around on its banks. For passengers going straight through to Wellington it was the beginning, the first chapter, of scenic New Zealand – the Overlander's twelve-hour journey is one of the world's great train rides. I viewed the river as the beginning of the end. Soon I would jump the Overlander's raft at Hamilton's railway station. It looked like it was held together with string and Sellotape. It was closed most of the day. It backed on to a field. Melancholy is always lovable, and I grew fond of the marooned station. I tromped over the field to work, or called a cab. The one-armed taxi driver, sometimes the taxi driver with his flatmate's dog in the back seat – Sit, Toby.

Going home was going backwards. First, the late afternoon light above the Waikato River; last, the night tide at Hobson Bay in Auckland. And then my daughter in pyjamas, ready for bed, running to the door: 'Daddy!' I kiss her mother. The house is warm and all the lights are on. Dinner is served. A happy ending. A happy day: the bright and amusing students at Wintec's school of journalism, where I am editor in residence, and the train. The rhythm of Tuesdays, the strangest and most vivid day of my working week.

I work from home. The train became another home, with its familiar comforts – the seats, the big windows, the low handles on doors. And there were the familiar faces of the Overlander attendants, who fussed over the passengers – apart from one abusive woman who got kicked off last month at Otorohonga and told to walk to Wellington. Jimmy has worked on the train for forty-five years, Bruce for thirty. 'It gets into your blood,' he said. Bruce wore an earring in his left ear, and read from his own script when he gave the onboard commentary. It was very funny. But his beard made him look like David Brent, and he said, 'I look upon myself as an entertainer.'

He talked about how the Overlander is parked in an enormous garage at the Otahuhu depot every night. Strange to think of it just sitting there, night and day, during the week over winter. Horrible to remember it was very nearly completely abandoned. Australian company Toll announced it would cease the Overlander service at the end of 2006. The decision was reversed at the eleventh hour, and Helen Clark's government bought Railways in 2008. National deny it will sell it back to private ownership. In the meantime, a hopeful petition with 11,000 signatures is calling for a regular service between Hamilton and Auckland, and there is excited talk about electrifying the line, allowing the train to boot the distance in an hour.

An hour! The river as a wet blur, the backyards of South Auckland gone in a flash. But I loved those steady, patient two hours and twenty minutes in late summer and autumn. The cactus plantation near Penrose, the pumpkin patches in Franklin, the Waikato workshop where staff sit outside for their morning smoko next to a battered World War II tank; the casual wander through the carriages, the chat and a laugh with attendants Simone, Tommy, Jimmy and Bruce. Daily service resumes for three weeks in the July school holidays. A temporary return to that Tuesday rhythm, that great good luck of commuting to and from work in a state of hypnosis, the train clinging to the tracks, forwards, backwards.

[May 16, 2010]

COLD DAYS IN HELL

The White Album

As usual, I am writing this column in a shed in my back-yard. There is the shade under the fig tree, and there is my daughter's Wendy house by the clothes line. Earlier today I saw kids swimming at Milford beach, and a man in a wheelchair who parked on the pavement outside a rest home in Avondale to smoke a cigarette. Today is the familiar laziness of summer in barefoot, undressed New Zealand, and when this column is published I will be in Antarctica.

I expect it will be cold. I daresay the landscape will look white. But I have no other idea where I am headed, or what I am in for. How can the imagination deal with the prospect of setting foot on that mad continent?

So many people have said to me, 'Oh, I've always wanted to go there.' It's never entered my head. The invitation came out of the blue, or the white. I got a call from Antarctica New Zealand on my cell phone over a year ago. It was a Friday afternoon just before Christmas, and that could mean only one thing for a man of my temperament. 'It's very good of you to ask,' I told the caller, 'but the fact of the matter is that right now I'm drunk in a bar.'

He thought that showed admirable presence of mind,

and said he would call again at a more convenient and sober hour. He did, a few weeks later, and this time I was able to make sense of what he was saying. I thanked him and said I would think about it. I gave it no further thought. Antarctica! Ridiculous.

Information about the continent is riddled with the most boring words in the English language – crampons, terrain, permafrost, insulator, crevasse, environment, tent. I loathe snow and dislike penguins. Scientific endeavour in the Antarctic has such a holiness and belligerence about it; Jenny Diski writes in her strange memoir *Skating to Antarctica*: 'The scientists have wrapped up an entire continent for their own and only their own purposes. ... Antarctica is in the control of the scientists as Mecca is under the authority of the mullahs.' Well, they can have it. All that barren expanse, the whole great big frozen lump.

The heroic age of Antarctic exploration by Scott, Shackleton and all the rest has never appealed, although my heart went out to Oates: he lost his pipe on the way to the South Pole. No tobacco in that wilderness – it really must have felt like the worst journey in the world. Oates perished on March 16, 1912, Scott thirteen or fourteen days later. It was less than a century ago, but it feels far more remote, from some ancient page in history. Oates' uncle was the fifth white man to see Victoria Falls; he died five weeks later, at thirty-four, with his cases of insects, reptiles and rare bird skins around him. Oates died at thirty-two. He had fought in the Boer

War; in the Antarctic he sang 'The Fly Be on the Turnip' on a banjo.

Scott's doomed party sailed to Antarctica from Dunedin. New Zealand has claimed an actual working presence on the continent since Edmund Hillary set up Scott Base in 1957. Then, having finished the job, he famously charged towards the South Pole on a Massey Ferguson tractor. Tremendous, but I have never wanted to follow in his footsteps to Everest either. Crampons, terrain, crevasse...

The one contemporary New Zealand link to Antarctica that everyone knows about is the incident on November 28, 1979 at Erebus. A few years ago I found Justice Peter Mahon's Royal Commission report in a second-hand bookstore. The original owner had folded in a column by Tom Scott from the May 16, 1981 issue of the *Listener*. The report had just been published; Scott's column reads as though it were written by a man in shock.

This may owe something to the fact that the report was – and is – a shocking read. Paragraph 398: 'The ultimate key to the tragedy lay in the white silence of Lewis Bay, the place in which the airliner had been unerringly guided by its micro-electronic navigation system, only to be destroyed, in clear air and without warning, by a malevolent trick of the polar light.'

The white silence. It's not merely a matter that Antarctica is the last place on Earth I've ever wanted to see. It's more the fact that Antarctica is the last place on Earth. The lost continent, the closest planet. Why go there? Why leave the long grass in my backyard? Why give up the easy pleasures of lush, civilised summertime?

The man from Antarctica New Zealand stayed in touch by email and phone. Months went by. I kept hedging. Finally he said that the deadline for an answer had arrived: Yes or no?

I thought about it. A fortnight in desolation. Snow, penguins, science... I phoned him back. He wasn't there. I left a message. I said: 'No.' And as soon as I put the phone down I felt sick as a parrot, empty, bloodless, a chicken. I had said no to something rare and amazing. I had said no to experiencing something that was completely beyond my comprehension or understanding or imagination. I had given the wrong answer. I phoned and left another message. I said: 'Yes, please.'

[January 18, 2009]

Daylight Saving in Antarctica

Before I travelled to Antarctica in January, I thought of it as the closest planet to Earth. But the truth was more far-fetched than that. It was an underworld, it was the devil's address – truly, I saw Hell. It was horrible, remorseless, madly in love with the idea of suffering; everything in it was frozen in agony, all hope abandoned, all speech incoherent. It was a genuine wasteland because it was non-existent, just a huge blank space. Hell, in January, is white.

But there are clocks in Hell, and this weekend Ross Island – that hard, dusty rock in Antarctica where New Zealand maintains Scott Base – conforms to daylight saving. Setting the clock back is unlikely to make any immediate difference to the light of Antarctica's blank space. Soon, though, darkness will creep over the horizon. Apparently it settles into a long dusk. By June it will be night, all the time.

Strange to think of it under a black sky. January was eternal sunshine, spotless, mindless. It did your head in. Most nights I was still wandering around the base at two a.m., sometimes later; sleep seemed lazy, an affront, when you looked out the window and only ever saw daylight. In fact the sky felt at its most cheerful at about two a.m. It had the quality of ten a.m., as though the day were raring to go. I would tiptoe into the kitchen, fix myself tea and toast, then step outside on to the smokers' deck. It looks out on to the shore. You could imagine it might be a pretty little seaside bay if global warming accelerated.

But there seemed no future to Antarctica, and no past. It looked as though it had never budged, only lain there, gigantic and monstrous, dedicated to nihilism. The sea was frozen. When it moved, it cracked and creaked. The temperature wasn't cold. It was beyond cold. You needed a new word for it but Antarctica wiped out language, had no interest in civilisation or love. It was pure evil in broad daylight.

I loathed it, couldn't wait to leave, and two days after I returned I was desperate to see it again. Plainly, Antarctica is an addictive substance. I met two workers at Scott Base who had clocked up one thousand nights on the ice. There was a definite feeling that you hadn't really spent any time on the continent until you'd wintered over. No planes in, no planes out – no exit until spring. Stuck there, locked down, looking up at the stars at breakfast, at lunch...

I often thought about food. It was the only thing on my mind whenever I walked to America. Ross Island is shared by New Zealand and the United States; McMurdo Station was a tortuous forty-five minute trot over the hill, and their mess did very good chicken. May I recommend the chicken pie, the chicken and lentil stew, and especially the barbecued chicken. The South Polar skua, a kind of hawk that quacks like a duck, tore down on anyone foolish enough to attempt a takeaway meal.

I saw a great many skuas on a field trip around Mount Erebus to Cape Bird. There is a two-bedroom hut on top of a hill above the beach; it's a fabulous resort, built in 1966 by carpenters Ray Greeks of Lower Hutt and Roger Bartlett from Warrington, Otago. They survived an Antarctic storm in that barren post, writing in the logbook: 'The roar of the wind and rattle of stones on the walls...' Even worse, in 1972 four University of Canterbury marine biology students – Jim Lowry, Paul Sagar, Warren Farrelly and Graeme Fenwick – were lost at sea when their boat drifted away from the shore. For fear the boat would be crushed by ice, they jumped on to a passing ice floe, and were adrift for five days until a rescue pilot caught 'a funny glint'.

The hut is close to a colony of 50,000 Adélie penguins screeching their heads off on pink mounds of excreted krill. They fished in the sea, they collected rocks, they lay on their stomachs; the skuas ate the young, and left behind only the flippers and feet once they had finished their amazing carnage. The ground was a vast open graveyard of flippers and feet. You couldn't walk two steps without treading on the dead. One end of the bay was closed off by a massive glacier. I would creep out of the hut and down to the shore to wander about the maddening noise and chaos at two a.m., sometimes later, in that circle of Hell exposed by daylight.

But I also decided to make myself useful. The cupboards

in the hut were stocked with obscure supplies that may well date back to the days of Ray Greeks. I whipped up pikelets, tried my hand at cheese scones, improvised a sweet cornflake biscuit, slaved over a Christmas pudding with custard. And then spaghetti bolognese, and a Thai-influenced beef dish. The hut was nice and warm, the view awful and stupendous. Strange to think of it about to succumb to darkness. I wonder what ten a.m. in June feels like at Cape Bird — black, cheerless, doomed? Antarctica takes itself so seriously. The end of daylight saving means the only two words that have meaning in the Antarctic: the end.

[April 5, 2009]

And They Are Warm

There will be a kind of funeral at Mount Erebus next weekend – summer in Antarctica, when there is no such thing as night, only an eternal sunshine of the spotless continent. A big, fat-bummed United States Air Force C-17 will leave Christchurch on Friday morning, and touch down at the Pegasus Field on Ross Island early that afternoon. The passengers will include five people who lost family on another summer's day thirty years ago, in that far-flung and far-fetched place.

First, though, a medical examination in New Zealand, including a battery of shots, and a test to determine colour-blindness, which involves looking at one of the most beautiful books ever published. The pages of Japanese ophthalmologist Shinobu Ishihara's watercolour charts are a wonder to behold, the lovely light colours dotted in soft, gentle mosaics – but the only colour in Antarctica is white, without beginning or end. It's a blank space. It seems only enormously pitiless. Mount Erebus wants to have a word with you: 'I am sorrow.' The line is by Bill Manhire, speaking for the mountain, in his poem about Erebus, and about what happened at Erebus. The next line: 'I am the debris trail.'

The passengers will be driven across ice and snow to nearby Scott Base, New Zealand's snug little home on the continent. They will be togged up in extreme cold-weather gear, issued before departure at a very strange men's and ladies' outfitter in Christchurch, on the premises of crown entity Antarctica New Zealand. The huge boots and criminal balaclavas, and the trousers, jackets and overalls festooned with cunning zips, are an essential comedy, and an easy New Zealand humour settles over everything at Scott Base. So, too, does the spirit of Ed Hillary, who helped build the place in 1957. A hut named after him has been set aside as a kind of museum. It contains priceless antiques – tins of Bournville cocoa, packets of Maggi turkey noodle soup.

There will be a safety briefing at Scott Base, and then a tour. The workshops, the dining room, the bunk rooms; it's pleasant to sit in the upstairs library a while, especially by the window, with a good book, at three a.m., when sleep seems like an affront to the continual broad daylight. The tour guide should also point out perhaps the most important feature at Scott Base: the outside porch for smokers. Air New Zealand flight TE901 on November 28, 1979 to Antarctica was so civilised that it had a smokers' section. Retrieved film of the flight shows people moving around, relaxed, frisky.

There, outside the front door of Scott Base, in no need of an introduction: Mount Erebus. It doesn't look like much. A hump, a small frozen lump. But flying over it, close up, it reveals enough of its outrageous massiveness to make you weak. At six p.m. on the day they arrive, the passengers will be taken by helicopter around the western slopes of Erebus to Lewis Bay – beneath an ice cliff, beneath the crash site, beneath a stainless steel cross – for a service conducted by Reverend Peter Beck, dean of Christchurch Cathedral.

The bar is likely to be open on Friday night. It might attract Scott Base staff – carpenters, electricians, mechanics – and scientists. Summer is the peak season of Antarctica New Zealand's science research programme. A team led by Craig Cary, a rather verbose American professor of biology at Waikato University, is right now studying microbial life in the superheated geothermal vents on top of Erebus. Next month, Dr Clive Evans of the School of Biological Sciences at Auckland University will arrive at Scott Base, and attempt to answer the question on everyone's lips: 'How do Antarctic fish use anti-freeze to survive in ice-laden waters?'

Saturday is the thirtieth anniversary of the tragedy that took all 257 lives onboard the DC10. Mourners will gather beside the New Zealand flagpole at Scott Base. A minute's silence will be observed at the exact time of impact: 12.49 p.m. Lunchtime on a summer's day in Antarctica, that white and amazing grave. Another line from Manhire's poem: 'And I am still a hand, a fingertip, a ring.' There are bodies on Erebus. A few years ago, parts of the plane's fuselage popped out of the snow – it was possible to see something blue, something green, and passenger windows.

Sunday is set down for a tour of someone else's tragedy –

a drive on a roaring Hagglund vehicle to Cape Evans, site of the hut built by doomed South Pole explorer Robert Falcon Scott. There are other options. Ross Island is a nice place for a walk. You can walk from New Zealand to America. It takes less than an hour to tromp over the hill from Scott Base to McMurdo Station, the US base, where there is a Wells Fargo ATM, and pink lemonade in the canteen.

Everywhere, sea ice, white light, wind, mad birds, impossible coldness. One more line from *Erebus Voices*, Manhire's poem, written in italics, speaking for the 257 dead: '*Yet we were loved and we are warm.*' Monday is the flight home. Away from that place where a plane crashed into a mountain, away from that weird, raw, frozen, alien but not entirely silent planet.

[November 22, 2009]

FATHER'S DAYS

Blonde Ambition

She is incandescent. Warm to the touch, as round and succulent as a little greased pig, a pagan idol chanting weird spells – she wakes up singing 'Happy to you' – she is, at nineteen months, in a state of grace, an occupant of a golden age. She has evicted the baby she used to be, that incompetent, gummy, staring bug, a prisoner of prams and high chairs, marooned at A without a hope of getting to B, and joined the biggest revolution of all our lives: behold, she walks among us.

An upright citizen, a determined troll out for a stroll. Watching my daughter walk can sometimes feel like a bigger miracle than birth; it's her own miracle, her own doing. It took her long enough. Until her first steps, she was either lazy or impractical, apparently content to crawl while her contemporaries got up on their hind legs, and loomed over her like ogres. I judged her severely. I served her a report that read: 'Distinctly below average.' But I also suspected she was covertly engaged in one of her inherited pastimes: sitting back, and watching.

Now that she has joined in, she is away laughing. I sit back, and watch, and wonder: do we ever truly experience an event as momentous as being able to stand on our own two feet? 'Well,' answers my fiancée, 'there's driving.' This is a tart and really quite frivolous comment aimed at the fact I can't and don't drive. But driving is only a minor rite of passage. Walking is major, a profound locomotion – our feet are a liberating army.

Set free, my daughter roams the wide open spaces: 'Plaza.' There, among the poor devils who sit for hours on end with six-packs of Cody's Colt Bourbon & Cola at their feet, she staggers and stumbles in her own fairly convincing impersonation of a town drunk, then bends down to take a close inspection at the joys of nature: 'Drain.'

I point out roadside signs: DANGER. ABRASIVE BURNING IN PROGRESS. She translates and says, 'Hot.' She is like an avid collector, scooping up words as she makes her rounds of the house, the garden, the plaza. 'Gentle.' 'Stuck.' 'Quiet.' 'Goddammit.' Her entire life is filled with the wonder of things, and also the naming of things. 'Umbrella.' 'Hose.' 'Lavender.' 'Newspaper.' Her entire world is on fire, a vivid blaze – a burning in progress. What colour is that tulip? 'Red.' Good. What colour is that lemon? 'Red.'

She is so nascent, an absolute beginner, a complete ignoramus. Her mind is there for the taking. I try and keep out of its way. Faith-based values have no place in her life, and neither does education, although I filled her music box with about a dozen words written on scraps of paper. 'Shoes.' 'Nana.' 'Off.' 'Duck.' The only word she claims to recognise is her own name. I dread the day when I have to break it to her that she also has a strange, ungainly surname. Her favourite toys are books – she is on close terms with such characters as Wibbly Pig, Messy Teddy and Wee Willie Winkie. At the library, she is happiest sitting by herself with a book in her lap; the book is upside down. Too young for the tyranny of Hannah Montana, thank God, she is nearly halfway to mastering the complete lyrics to 'Twinkle, Twinkle'.

We travel to distant lands. Together, we sail the seven seas of Auckland by bus, and set foot on the shores of Karanga-hape Road. She walks into the Hare Krishna Food for Life restaurant, where rather sour staff serve her semolina with custard. She trudges past Artspace Gallery, where a new exhibition is advertised by a sign that reads: PLASTIC IS LEATHER, F**K YOU. She sings, 'Up above the world so high.'

An innocent abroad, a sensualist who wants her face mopped with a warm cloth, who stops at the florist to smell the flowers. She is on close terms with goodness. Resolutely cheerful, she greets strangers on the street, approaches babies with a question: 'Cuddle?' Her tantrums are few and brief. She is as fit as any number of fiddles, sleeps like any number of logs. She could eat a horse, but will accept broccoli. She has no doubt that the cow does in fact jump over the moon. She lends a helping hand to fill bowls of water with three spoons of sugar for tui and silvereyes, and says, 'Sugarbirds.'

Parents of older children say: Oh, it just gets better and better. I can believe it. Sitting back and watching her grow up will be a blessing. But right now is her golden age, her age of innocence, full of the joys of legging it. At nineteen months old, suspended in sunlight, just another New Zealand pedestrian hogging the pavement, unable to dress herself, a fat fool, executing dance steps to 'We Belong Together' by Mariah Carey before bedtime, in her pyjamas by seven, in love with her cousins, in clover, neither fearless nor impulsive, a cool customer, steady as she goes, dispensing kindness at the drop of a hat, observant, alert, tender, incorruptible, totally harmless, completely happy, she is immaculate – the owner of a golden heart.

[October 12, 2008]

Christmas Baby

She is going to love Thursday. Family, presents, meat, a tree with lights. Also, she will be able to put her feet up and slop around the house. Christmas marks a special event in her 2008 calendar. She started her first job back in February; at nearly two years old, she is about to experience the joys of annual leave.

Three days every week, she trudges into work. I go with her; three days every week, I step inside an enchanted forest. Where the wild things are, small, furry, random, spouting cheerful nonsense – the predictable adult world evaporates, is left behind the moment I tap out the security code at the door. Abandon rational thought, all ye who enter. It makes no difference to most of the inmates. They have never owned a rational thought in their lives. I love day care.

Community leaders and other bores are fond of declaring, 'Children are our future.' But children are so old-fashioned. Their day-care lives are still played out like characters in *The Famous Five*; they have ever such fun. They scheme, they act on pure whim, they leave what they're doing and wander off in a narcotic daze. The girls fuss over dolls; the boys study principles of applied engineering as they sit down on the floor with train sets. There are times when I look around at day care and assume I have arrived in the nineteenth century.

I never want to leave. I stick around for about half an hour while my rampant and round-bellied daughter settles in for the day. She is already a seasoned campaigner, wise to the ways of the sandpit. But is it in her best interests? The new minister of social welfare, Paula Bennett, who is fast shaping up as one of New Zealand's most prominent vacant lots, recently announced that she wants a national debate about parents who place their kids in day care. 'I don't think we've had that debate as a society about what it means,' she blathered. Where, she wants to know, does it leave the children?

My daughter is available for comment. Midnight's good. She wakes up most nights at that hour, seized with a sudden desire to discuss current events. 'Olive changed nappies.' Oh, yes? 'No hitting, Nicole.' No. 'Stop it, Julia! Don't, Julia!' Good heavens. And so on, avidly sharing the latest absorbing melodramas – day care is her *Coronation Street* in miniature.

Her commentary would enliven Bennett's debate, but there are other louder, more juvenile voices wanting to be heard. Bob McCroskie is already one of New Zealand's most prominent vacant lots; the Family First lobbyist thinks the notion of a debate is 'brilliant'. It would allow him further opportunity to express his belief that a mother's place is in the home. No, I've no idea why his views are sought by the media either. Still, he may be getting his wish. There was a leaving party for a girl at day care a few weeks ago. Her mother had lost her job. Two other children have been taken out of day care due to redundancies.

Everyone there was born in the Helen Clark years. They are now children of the recession, and will inherit whatever change of education policy and whatever tender mercies are served up by the new government. Good luck to all concerned. It's a great day-care centre. I have heard anecdotal reports of other centres run like boot camps, where desolate children are left to rot on beanbags for hours on end, where cynical staff show affection only in front of parents. My daughter got lucky. I hold her teachers in awe.

Gentle, attentive, smart, they swoop down on violent offenders, and pass a coded message to each other: 'No language.' It seems to be a form of preventive justice, and it works. They sing, they cuddle, they instruct; they talk about the need for privacy, the importance of respecting one another; they are holding the fort of political correctness. Good. I once heard that a teacher asked a truculent boy, 'Are you making the right decisions?' I always regard such questions as a form of torture but it stopped him in his tracks. The children do the madness; the staff do the method.

But the children are the stars. Their company is dazzling. I love their intent faces, the workings of their ridiculous and beautiful minds. A serious little boy sat next to me one afternoon and began to ask a question. 'Is ... um ... is ... is she ... um...' He was pointing at my daughter. I stroked his hair and waited for him to find the words. It was worth it. He asked, 'Is she your darling?'

In 2008 she has learned to talk and walk, often at the same time. She flew to Nelson for a wedding and saw a peacock. She rode a bus to Karangahape Road. She asked to sleep with a photo of her cousins. She worried that tigers might climb trees. She fell off a trampoline. She fell in love with every baby she saw. She fell into early childhood. And she went to work, where she took down names and brought them out at midnight, sitting on the living-room couch in darkness with her mother and father: every day with her is Christmas Day.

[December 21, 2008]

Fairlie, Population 751

Tomorrow I will be in Darfield. The fun starts there: tomorrow marks the first day of a week-long South Island author tour set up by that august body the New Zealand Book Council, which every year promotes a road trip called Words on Wheels. The idea is to bring New Zealand literature into the community. And so for the next week I will be stuffed inside a hire van with a poet, a novelist, a playwright and an author of young adult fiction, and together we will operate under the guise of travelling minstrels who appear in public places to provide something which may or may not resemble wild entertainment.

We will read out loud from our books. In return, there will be morning tea in schools, and supper in community halls. Milk, no sugar, please. Is there any more cake? I have an even healthier appetite for mooching about in quiet towns, and look forward to the van spilling me out to wander the several streets of Darfield, then south to Methven, Geraldine, Twizel, Wanaka – no sleep 'til Cromwell. The yellow hills of late summer, the exchange of pleasantries on clean pavements. ... But there is one other destination I'm especially excited about: Fairlie.

Research probably shows that no one in New Zealand history has ever claimed they were excited at the prospect of visiting Fairlie. It's a modest, tidy settlement that lies close to the ground in the Mackenzie Country. The main street is called Main Street. It has a river, two pubs and a thriving cemetery. Its population in the 2001 census was 753, with 97.1 percent attesting they were European, and 20.3 percent aged over sixty-five. Back then, all those figures would have included my father.

He lived in Fairlie for about ten, fifteen years. A comical Austrian in moccasins and snug jerseys, happy in his home with the sliding doors opening to a porch with a view of the Two Thumbs Range, offering his familiar cheerful greeting on the clean pavements of Main Street: 'Mein herr!' It was our habit to play pool at the pub in nearby Kimbell, and observe the mounted 43-pound salmon caught by an L. Rooney in 1970. We would drive further, sometimes to Kurow, where he would stop at the butcher shop for smoked and pickled tongue. I had no desire to put that tongue anywhere near my mouth but it was a firm favourite with Eunice.

All the loves of his life wore antique names – Doris, Eunice, Dolly. Eunice was his second wife. They had met in Mount Maunganui and left town, and their marriages, as scandalised lovers. Fairlie was a kind of exile, a safe distance from their past. It's true that for several years I viewed Eunice as a grotesque creature, but I grew up and came to know her as a dear soul and an antic spirit, hilarious, sensitive, coarse, melancholic, who played up a storm on the piano and played merry hell whenever her mood turned to distemper. She spoke in a harsh croak, but there was a music in her voice, a distant melody. She could be adorable; the very least anyone said in her favour was that she was a colourful presence.

As a couple they shouted and roared, although this was partly due to bad hearing. At night, the TV was turned up so loud that the walls hummed. Eunice would scowl at the screen, hissing insults at actors, newsreaders, weather presenters, and finally retire to bed in a huff. But there were nights of insomnia. She would get up, pad the kitchen floor in slippers, then settle into an armchair, where she would scowl at crosswords. Once, she burst open the door to the spare room where I was sleeping and demanded, 'Who wrote *Great Expectations?*'

Two or three in the morning in a flat South Island town hemmed in by tussock and snow, and the sudden apparition of an immense figure in a nightgown wishing to know the author of a masterpiece. Outside, the town as dead as its cemetery, the river trickling past the camping ground, moonlight on the digits of the Two Thumbs Range. Inside, a cuckoo clock, white lace curtains, the walls decorated with my father's landscape paintings of yellow hills in summer, a fridge stocked with tongue, and a dialogue that resembled wild farce.

In a feeble, frightened voice, I volunteered that the answer to her question was Charles Dickens. She replied in her singsong croak, 'Who? Speak up!' Charles DICKENS. Again, the harsh melodious voice in the darkness: 'Who? Louder!' CHARLES! DICKENS! Again: 'Who?' Just as I began to despair that I was doomed to chant the name of Charles Dickens all night, my father hollered from his bed: 'Will the two of you shut up!'

So ended the Charles Dickens quiz. It remains one of the most vivid literary conversations I have experienced. It would be a vain hope to inspire anything as memorable when I appear in Fairlie on Thursday night, posing as an author on tour, just grateful for the opportunity to return to that clearing in the tussock, to that town where I loved two people now no longer there, no longer anywhere.

[March 1, 2009]

The Veteran of Point Chevalier

They grow up slow. She turned two in February. Even though she doubled her age overnight, getting there took forever. Children only look small. They are big, heavy bears, larger than life, as difficult to shift as a piano. They fill up the day, hog it. The past is beaten into submission, takes the form of myth and legend. And now she marvels at her own ancient history. 'I used to be,' she says, 'a baby.'

She used to sleep in a pram and sit strapped in a high chair. Both vehicles are now parked at the back of the garage, as obsolete as typewriters, weird and improbable relics. She used to wear bibs. They are stored in a dry, limp heap in a kitchen cupboard. She used to stand only as high as the lowest pencil mark I sketched on the trellis on our back porch. It was made when she was less than a month old, and it looks like some sort of prank, as though I were measuring the height of a cat.

We talk a lot about the past. I tell her the same stories over and over, usually about acts of random violence and swift punishment. The time we were at the beach, when a boy kicked water in her face, she cried, and I yelled at the brute, 'What the hell do you think you're doing?' Or the time we were in a playground, when a boy threw a hard plastic toy at her, she took no particular notice, and I roared at the savage, 'What the hell do you think you're doing?'

But all of it – the pram, the bibs, the morality tales – seem so far-fetched. Her presence is absolute: it leaves no room for the past or the future. She is only who she is every second. Permanent, complete, ageless, built to last. I can never imagine her a day older or a day younger. She is the little girl who sits on the floor with a book in her lap. She is the little girl who refuses to wear this skirt or that top, throws them down, and announces: 'These clothes are angry!' She is the little girl who could never have been a baby.

The facts contradict it. I can lay my hands on documentary evidence. All I have to do is pause at the fridge door and look at a photo of her taken when she was a fat lump, dark-haired and dozing, aged less than a week. I can see a curious resemblance to the little girl who can spell her first name and even pronounce her surname, who uses her hands to climb ladders, open doors, and brush her blonde hair from her face, but the dazzling and exhilarating present annihilates faint memories of the baby she once, apparently, used to be.

Children are as brilliant as flames. You can't take your eyes off them. And you're not even aware – the fact escapes you, slips through your fingers – that their past drifts and curls away with every passing second. It disappears. They continue burning. 'You've been coming here all your life,' I tell her when we visit the local tea room and share our usual table. She knows what to expect: 'Daddy has a hot cup.' She greets staff by their names. She is a familiar face, a stately antique – you could measure out her life in coffee spoons. But she kills nostalgia dead with a single glance. She is only ever contemporary, *du jour*.

She catalogues her moods, states astonishing facts, finds work for idle hands. 'I'm a bit shy ... Gooses don't wear nappies ... Shall we build a tower?' She builds her own civilisation with language, art, music. She thinks all men with beards look like the drawing of Mr McGregor in Beatrix Potter's books; she listens only to female singers – Alanis, Stevie, Lucinda. She leads a full life. For something to do on a wet day, I took her on the train to Glen Innes. She eats her greens. When she cries, she says, 'Hot tears.' She rides a pink tricycle – one day I'll have to pack that away in the garage. She attended a wedding in Upper Moutere, got lost in Te Papa. When she wakes up in her cot, she lies on her back and makes long speeches. Her legs are covered in bruises from falls. Her paper lantern caught on fire at the Lantern Festival. But she won't remember a thing, not even Glen Innes.

And so I bring out the myths and morality tales, give her lessons in ancient history. I tell her that when she was a baby, her mother and I would check on her before we went to bed, and usually find her asleep on her stomach at the foot of the cot, on top of her blankets, as though she had been trying to escape and collapsed with the effort. She was in that exact position on the last night she was one year old. I picked her up and shovelled her inside the blankets without waking her. 'Happy birthday, darling,' we said to her in the morning, the first morning her age became a plural. I don't think she's attempted to escape from her cot ever since.

[May 10, 2009]

Watching Iggle Piggle

She loves TV. She has two favourite shows. They both play on TV2. She is the channel's target audience. Just about everything on TV2, as its name suggests, appeals to the mental age of a two year old. *Fear Factor*, *Shortland Street*, *Ghost Whisperer*, *Desperate Housewives*, *Mitre 10 Dream Home*... But she is judicious and prefers *In the Night Garden* and *Yo Gabba Gabba!*

They screen each weekday morning. Fresh from her cot, she sits all blonde and vague on the blue couch, swigs on a bottle of warm milk, and eventually asks, 'Shall me and you watch *In the Night Garden*?' I reply, 'That's a good idea! I'd love to!' The truth is that I mean it. The fact is that I am losing my mind.

In the Night Garden is voiced by Derek Jacobi. Yes, the same Derek Jacobi who played the lead role in the land-mark BBC series *I, Claudius*, and who is regarded as one of England's greatest living Shakespearean stage actors. That beautifully trained voice now says, 'Somebody's not in bed! Who's not in bed? Iggle Piggle's not in bed!' And then Iggle Piggle falls over. Derek Jacobi probably does, too.

Iggle Piggle is blue. He is incapable of speech, but he

emits a fairly expressive squeak. He is the anchorman of *In the Night Garden*. Each episode opens with Iggle Piggle sailing a boat at night. It transports him up into the stars, and thence inside a sunlit garden, where soft little creatures — Makka Pakka, Upsy Daisy, the Tombliboos — enjoy soft little adventures. It's a lovely show, very sweet, quite slow, and perhaps intolerably boring. I have heard other parents complain that nothing ever happens. But there was high drama when Makka Pakka lost his uff-uff.

Makka Pakka lives in a cave. He has soft little habits, which include an insistence on washing stones with soap and a sponge, and then drying them with an appliance called an uff-uff. One day it got knocked out of his hands by a bouncing ball, flew in the air, and landed in Upsy Daisy's bed. Jacobi: 'Oh dear!' It marked the show's only known instance of violence.

But there could be many hidden instances of sex. It's hard to trust the English in these matters, with their secrets and lies, their love of concealed smut. Jacobi: 'Upsy Daisy loves her bed!' Also: 'Upsy Daisy loves Iggle Piggle!' They kiss on the lips, hold each other tight. She wears a kind of mini-skirt. The hem rises when she's excited, and you can see her knickers. There was a notorious episode when Iggle Piggle climbed into Upsy Daisy's soft little bed. His squeaks were more expressive than usual.

Each character, played by desperate actors inside sealed costumes, performs a signature song and dance. 'Yes,' sings

Jacobi, 'my name is Iggle Piggle!' Oh dear. *I, Iggle Piggle*. They dance together at the end of every episode. In a gazebo. The gazebo twirls around and around. Slowly. Computer-animated birds – toucans, hoopoes, white-cheeked turacos – whistle a goodnight song from a tree. Everyone goes to bed. Not quite everyone. 'Somebody's not in bed!' etc. Monday, Tuesday, Wednesday... We snuggle together on the blue couch, ogling at Iggle Piggle, our thoughts slowly twirling around and around in our soft little minds.

Apart from the suspect nature of Upsy Daisy, that giddy sensual imbecile, *In the Night Garden* is dreamy and innocent. It has quaint, dozy, impeccably English virtues. *Yo Gabba Gabba!* is dazzling, fast, inventive, lively, brazen, cool – obviously it's American. You could describe it as a variety show. You could just as easily describe it as a cultural event.

It gathers some of the best talent in America. The host is DJ Lance, a tall, elastic black guy who dances to hip-hop beats. Guest stars include Elijah Wood, Jack Black and Rhys Darby. There is music by bands such as The Ting Tings, Smoosh and The Postmarks, whose performance of 'I Love Balloons' is the best new pop song I've heard this year. A guy called Mark appears most episodes and shows how to draw a sketch. He used to be in Devo. As a film composer, he wrote the musical score for *The Royal Tenenbaums*.

Dazzling, etc. Happily, though, it relies on soft little creatures. Desperate actors inside sealed costumes play a core ensemble of a robot, a cat, a kind of pig, a long-armed green thing and a one-eyed orange thing. They sing, they dance, they talk. The quality of their singing, dancing and talking is very, very clever. I ask her, 'Can I watch *Yo Gabba Gabba!* with you?' She replies, 'If you want to.'

I almost resent the show's brilliance. *Yo Gabba Gabba!* is the outside world, busy and vibrant, talented and smart. She's starting to like it a lot more than *In the Night Garden*. The day is coming when she'll entirely reject that show's non-verbal English charms, and won't watch it at all. I'll miss Iggle Piggle, Makka Pakka, Upsy Daisy and the Tombliboos like mad. When they disappear from our life, they'll take her soft little childhood with them.

[July 12, 2009]

Twenty-four O'Clock in September

She asks her mother, 'How many words are there?' And then: 'Has anybody counted all of them up?' We are fascinated by her ease with language, but love her for her tremendous stupidity. At two and a half, plump, waddling, half-baked, she knows more or less nothing about anything. With her golden hair, she is like a blonde joke, her dim empty head seized with fancies, excitements, whims, indignations, vanities, hilarities, moral outrages, and other impulses. Good. The lessons and conformities of a New Zealand education can wait. She exists as entirely herself, a noble savage, an adorable dimwit.

Right now is her pre-school, pre-intellectual time of wild surmise and familiar certainties, the world close at hand, every possibility in reach. 'Shall we go to Saturn? But,' she says, 'you have to sit next to me.' She points at the deckchair in the backyard. We squeeze in together, side by side, and she begins the countdown to blast-off. 'Eight! Three! Sixty-fifteen!'

All children are great twits. She is years away from knowing how to tie her shoelaces, or tell the time – 'It's twenty o'clock four,' she declares. You expect strange and appealing fabrications, and you get strange and appealing fabrications. Children always play with a full deck of lies. She slings a purse over her arm, and announces, 'I'm just going up to the shops to buy twenty dollars.'

'Okay, gorgeous. What else will you buy?'

'A gate.'

'That's useful. Anything else?'

'A waterfall.'

And then she waddles out of the lounge and into the kitchen, singing.

Our fear is that she will take up the family trade and lower herself to become – please God, no – a journalist. Her questioning is precise, serious. She observes, has an eye for detail. Also, she misquotes. One day, exhausted by carrying her in my arms up to the shops, I said, 'God almighty.' She said, 'Did you say, "I got a nightie"?'

She likes fact as much as fantasy, but I do my best to fill her head with nonsense. My role model as a parent might be Lewis Carroll's father. When he was seven, Carroll wrote asking his father to return from Leeds with a present. His father's reply described his terrible wrath if the shops were closed: 'I will leave nothing but one small cat alive in the whole town of Leeds. Then what a bawling and tearing of hair there will be! Pigs and babies, camels and butterflies, rolling in the gutter together – old women rushing up chimneys and cows after them, ducks hiding themselves in coffee cups and fat geese trying to squeeze themselves into pencil cases...' The letter could serve as a kind of introduction to Carroll's masterpiece, *Alice's Adventures in Wonderland*.

And so I tell her about tigers in caves at the local creek, and hoist her over my shoulder and inform her she is a sack of potatoes that needs to be thrown on to the bed, because the bed is a ship, and the ship is about to sail on a long voyage – the usual inventions. And then I say to her, 'Hey.'

'Mmmm?'

'I really, really love you.'

'Oh, that's very nice of you, Father.' She is Victorian, full of stiff little formalities. And then she says, 'You say, "Giddy aunt." That's a funny word, isn't it?'

'I completely agree with you.'

'And what do you say I am?'

'How do you mean, sweet cat?'

'You say, "Clumsy oaf!" And "Hooligan!" Hooligan's a funny word.'

'Yes. And I also call you "Big lump". What do you call me?'

'I don't know.'

'You say, "Silly old guy." Poor Father!'

'Don't cry.'

'You're a good daughter.'

I give her a kiss. And then she skips away, and says, 'You're a fat Hottentot egg.' It's comforting to think of her merely as a cheerful imbecile, but she has an acute knowledge of melancholy. On an afternoon at the park, she sits listlessly on the swing. I ask her if she's all right. She says in a small voice, 'I'm feeling a bit sad.'

I hold her tight. 'Let's go home, darling.' We walk away in silence. After a few minutes, I put her down, look into her eyes, and ask her what she's thinking about. She says, 'I was thinking about when I was sad at the park.'

'I was thinking about that, too.'

'I just need a rest, and sit on the blue couch with my mummy and my daddy.'

'You bet.' I stroke her face. She is mysterious and profound. And then she smiles, and says, 'What I can smell?'

'I don't know, love.'

'Animal pooh.'

'Good lord.'

'Oh my giddy aunt,' she says.

[September 27, 2009]

Summer Baby

She has been longing for Friday all year – her first Christmas as a word, as a knowledge, as a promise. She was beside herself when the tree arrived, and the decorations went up, and the lights were switched on. 'It glows,' she swooned, and ran around the house, her fat feet slapping the floor. At two, she is in full possession of the Christmas facts: the reindeer, the elves, the biscuit and the glass of milk; the reward for good behaviour; the desolation that punishes naughtiness. Jesus has a minor role. Another, more cheerful myth looms over everything – December's god of avarice, ripe as a plum, who sits on his bum all day in shopping malls. She respects Santa's authority. She is a greedy little pig.

It will probably rain on Friday. But it will be a day of wonder and ice cream, possibly even love. Like all children, she is the reverse of modern surgery – a greedy little pig inserted with a human heart. There was one strange, miraculous stretch that lasted something like six weeks when she was only ever sunny. She was like a satire of goodness. She lavished her affections, she whooped it up, she made great art, she said please and thank you, she passed on compliments; she never complained, never whined; she woke up laughing and she went to sleep smiling. It was like living with a born-again Christian. We looked on, grateful and amazed, near speechless. 'She glows,' we swooned. She was golden weather. Golden weather always ends. Complaint and whining eventually resumed its head-splitting broadcast. All children are fucking brats.

It only gets worse, and it only gets better. A friend, a mother of three, said: Kids have their own childhood. I said: What? At two, her parents own her childhood. She knows her place. 'Home, sweet home,' she says. And, with deep satisfaction: 'Just the three of us. No one else.' But also, sadly: 'I wish I had a sister.' An only child, or so far, she is aware of her status as the one small person in the house, and can carry her age like a disappointment. One of her few precocities is already knowing how to mope.

A sensitive flower, a belligerent ape; adorable, appalling; hilarious, repetitive – in short, an average New Zealand specimen of her age. The charming and the gormless blend in at her day care, which she attends two days a week. Last year she had to be dragged away; for quite a lot of the time this year she's hated the thought of it. Fair call. There are mornings when the place seems a complete shambles. All children are lunatics, but they don't want to take over the asylum. She cries, she begs: 'Don't go! Five more minutes, okay?' It's unpleasant to feel like the worst parent in the world. But there she is in the afternoon, jovial and calm, looked after and vaguely educated, a bright spark holding her latest clutch of day-care paintings. She dances over the motorway bridge and past the Mad Butcher, the RSA and the Shell, until she gets to her home in a flat suburban street. White picket fence out front, strawberry patch out back.

Made in New Zealand, and a citizen of the modern world. 'Email,' she says. 'DVD.' 'iPod.' And: 'Charli Delaney, Nathan Foley, Sun Park, Stevie Nicholson, Kelly Hoggart.' I love it when she recites the hallowed names of the cast who sing, badly, and banter, in violently Australian accents, each weekday morning on *Hi-5*. Speculating about the cast dynamics – nice, dim Kelly loathes that self-centred bitch Charli, you can just tell – is the only way for an adult to survive *Hi-5*. But it starts her day. It's one of her necessary routines, like the Friday treat at McDonald's. Pointing at the figure of the store's famous mascot, that lipsticked simpleton in a clown suit, she asks, 'Daddy, who's the lady?'

I love her voice. I love her thoughtfulness, her eyelashes, her composure, everything. I love the sight of her with her mother, the powerful feminine display of the brunette voluptuary with beautiful legs holding on tight to the blonde child in pink pyjamas. I love her acceptable fatness, her flair for a good sentence. She makes up stories in the bath. 'It was summertime and it was raining,' she says, setting an Auckland scene. 'The people went to the shop. They said, "Let us in!" But the man said, "No." The people said, "Oh. Why?" And the man said, "Because you are too naughty." And everybody had a great time. The end.'

The beginning. Her first anticipation of Christmas, but there's something else that she's longed for since winter, something more important – summer. Her litany is practised, excited. 'In summer,' she says, 'you eat watermelon, and just wear singlets, and play with the hose, and go to the beach.' Summer is the great theme of New Zealand childhood. At two, three in February, she worships the idea of summer-time, its easy pleasures, its barbecues and togs. All children deserve the world. Sunshine is a gift everyone can share. I hope she stuffs herself with it, runs squealing towards it, tanned and blonde and glowing. Golden weather.

[December 20, 2009]

Emily

She is, from today, the mother of a three-year-old daughter. The birthday party should actually be in her honour. It's possible the daughter might object, and there's always Mother's Day. But that date seems as though it's picked out of a hat. It doesn't even have a date. It's less important than Valentine's Day, Anzac Day and Christmas Day; it's merely set down for the second Sunday in May. The Americans dreamed that up, in the same way they made Thanksgiving a moveable feast. The revolution starts here. In this house, quietly, discreetly, so as not to upset the star attraction, it's today.

She should get a present. What do you give the woman who gave everything on this date three years ago? She survived that colossal hospital drama, the useless, dangerous advice of a wretched midwife, the rescue operation by trained health professionals. The instruments, the smocks; and then some very good words: 'We have a baby.'

A happy ending. It began the previous night. It was hard labour. The father was there, an irrelevant presence, pale and stunned – he can more easily remember the late-night drive to the hospital along Karangahape Road, haggard prostitutes waving for business on dark corners. He thought: please let her grow up to choose a better career. In hospital all he thought was: please let her grow up.

Ancient history. At three years old, the daughter is agile and marauding, blonde and delirious. 'I used to be a baby.' And: 'It's twenty o'clock.' Also: 'Tigers! Quick, hide!' The mother is lovely and serene, mostly, despite the daughter's moods, the father's moods, her own moods – he swears there are times when it's like living with a teenager. War is declared one second, love the next. There are sudden rebellions, terrible threats, unexpected adorations. He makes wild claims that he's the head of the household. In reality, he's run ragged by the two females of the species but he's a willing hostage. He knows he's on to a good thing.

He wanted her the second he met her. Her beauty – those eyes, that body – took over the room, cleared it. He asked her out, they kissed in a bar. Five years ago – her other life, single, on the town. She lived in a city apartment, walked to her office. Intense, unsmiling Indians slammed the exit door along the corridor. There was an outrageous pink suit – tight skirt, three-button jacket – in her wardrobe. They dined at the French Café on her birthday, stayed the night in a suite at the Langham Hotel. They took epic road trips up to the North Cape and around the East Coast, in motels, on beaches, their togs drying on the back seat, Bob Marley, Sigur Rós and Jackson Browne on the car stereo. Summer lovers.

He got lucky, she got him. And then they got a daughter. Three years as a mother, three years of happiness beyond compare. The cot, the bassinet, the pram; and now the swimming lessons, the nail polish, the wild claims: 'Do you know, I gave my Barbie a bath, and washed her hair, and wrapped her in a towel, and she said "Bullshit." That's very naughty of her.' Also, the thoughtful interludes. Father and daughter sit quietly together on the porch; she eats a pear and asks, 'What are you thinking about?' He says, 'Oh, just a story I was writing. What are you thinking about?' She says, 'Pears.'

And so on, articulate and exhausting, a good girl, sensitive, comic, typical, in love with singlets, her cousins, vanilla ice cream. The worst thing she's ever done is smear toothpaste on the heater. But child-raising is never just one thing: it's one thing after another, leaving the parents exhausted, inarticulate.

Life is elsewhere, occasionally. The parents sometimes do go out. The movies, three or four times a year; less than that to a restaurant that isn't a food hall. Mostly, they are far less Mick and Bianca than Paul and Linda, domestic drudges on their Mull of Kintyre, stuck at home with a kid in an Auckland suburb. In a rare appearance at a party, he'll roll with the vodka punch and take over the dance floor. Afterwards, he asks her: 'Did I dance all right?' She replies: 'Well, you were prolific.' And while he busts his very old moves, she'll get hit on.

She's hot, looks sexy in tight skirts and an unbuttoned shirt. Her bedside table is scattered with Chomsky, Nietzsche ('Ah, women. They make the highs higher and the lows more frequent'), Alice Munro, Linda Goodman, *Yoga Journal*, *NW* magazine ('Brad begs Ange LET ME GO!'). She dances in the house, runs out the door and leaps over the porch for the silliness of it. She spends hours on the phone with her mouthy best friend in Wellington, vows she'll resign, soon, from the inane domain of Facebook. She spends ages in the shower, runs late, jogs, blends carrot drinks, composts, paints her nails; she's in her thirties, she's a teenager.

He's somewhat older. He has a dimly remembered past, she has a bright future. It joins together in the present. Today is the day of balloons, cake, fizz; today is the day to celebrate two sweethearts – a girl, a woman.

[February 21, 2010]

THE STATE WE'RE IN

A Country Wedding

They flew in from Perth, from Melbourne, from Christchurch, from Wellington, to attend a country wedding on the outskirts of Piako County. It was winter the day of the wedding, and spring the next. On Whitaker Street in Te Aroha, a shop sign read: IRREGULAR HOURS DUE TO CALVING SEASON. On the Piako plain, lightly garlanded with white magnolia and pink cherry blossom, a road sign read: CUSTOM KILLING.

The wedding was held in the chapel of an Anglican boarding school. At the school gates, a girl on horseback said, 'Just follow the road around to the right.' There was a statue of an owl in the school gardens. It looked put out about its station in life – in shadow, and exposed to a stiff breeze. But it had not budged during the three storms of July and August. Winds as fast as 200 kilometres an hour howled through the county; to the west, a trampoline flew from a lawn and lodged twelve metres up a macrocarpa tree; in Te Aroha, twelve homes lost their roofs. Rainfall had raised the Waihou, Waitoa and Piako rivers. Pasture was still under water.

The chapel felt like a narrow and tidy hut. The chapel organ sounded as warm as a fire. There came the bride, and two flower girls. The bride wore a veil. The groom was crammed inside a waistcoat. The vows were from Paul: 'Love believes all things, hopes all things, endures all things.' It was a brief, elegant ceremony and the Anglican rites worked their old familiar magic. There were loud cheers as bride and groom walked back down the thin aisle as man and wife, radiant, exhilarated, transformed, joined. They looked brand new, two banknotes stamped and hot off the press for use as legal tender.

The economy was in a recession; the Beijing Olympics had started; Russia and Georgia went to war. But the day was devoted to the happiness of two people on the outskirts of Piako County. Two or three hundred guests came to bear witness. After the ceremony, they stood in weak sunshine outside the chapel and said, 'The last time I saw you was at a funeral.' And: 'Come on, dear. Let's get you out of the cold.' Also: 'Doesn't she look beautiful?'

There was a human rights lawyer who had recently returned from Afghanistan. There was a woman who had changed her name because she was apparently on a spiritual journey. There was a man whose cell phone rang during the ceremony. There was a novelist, a builder, an environmental waste consultant, and a semi-retired journalist. They drove from the chapel to a vineyard, past water towers and over railway lines. Three people stood on the verandah of a shack and waved out to the wedding party driving by in vintage automobiles on a sharp afternoon in winter.

A land of three rivers, of fern birds in the peat swamps. The ground is thick with bloodstock and livestock – the last census counted 368,237 head of cattle – and fat with milk, butter and cream. Pastoral, serene, lovely, but police raided two P-labs in Te Aroha in December, and on November 15 a seventy-nine-year-old Cambridge man, facing thirty-three counts of sexual offending against young boys, was found dead in the Te Aroha mineral pools. He had had a massive heart attack. On the day of his death, he had been contacted by police about fresh charges, and phoned his daughters in a 'distressed state'. The family said media accusations had made his life intolerable. His lawyer said that a former police officer had been jailed for blackmailing the man and pocketing $120,000 in hush money.

'Raise your glasses!' And glasses were raised and raised and raised and raised again, as toasts were led by family and friends at the vineyard. There was a table for presents. Waiters offered plates of crumbed prawn cutlets. The sit-down meal was crowned with spit-roast lamb and dark gravy. Speakers told stories of the couple's separate pasts – a holiday in Corsica, an incident in Twizel. Everything was revealed. The bride cried. The groom cried. Their lives had flashed before them, and led to the stunning flash of this very moment, of this happy ending. A bridesmaid said, 'They have a sunny and nutty optimism.' And then glasses were raised once more, and the band played.

At day or night, from north or south, one of the greatest

drives in New Zealand is towards Te Aroha. The roads —
Scotsman Valley Road, No 1 Road, No 2 Road — zig and
zag in straight lines on the Piako plain, with the destination
always in sight. Mount Te Aroha raises itself up, gently, and
the town rests in its lap, held like a precious jewel. In a storm,
the wind drops off the top of the mountain and races across
the plain; on the Sunday morning after the wedding, Mount
Te Aroha looked warm to the touch, a cauldron boiling with
the town's famous mineral waters.

Somewhere beyond the river flats and the peat swamps,
it was the first morning of the rest of their lives for the
couple who held a perfect wedding on the outskirts of Piako
County. The sky was entirely blue. There was a light frost.
Love believes all things.

[August 24, 2008]

Rain

We were walking around the neighbourhood in the rain when we saw a banana plant that looked like it was rotten to the core, its leaves peeling and shredded, and she said, 'That's Auckland for you – a tropical dump.'

South, they get snow and ice, floods and slips, drought and blight. Grim conditions, with the howl of a high wind in the trees, the mountains in sharp and fierce silhouette. Brian Turner will put it into verse, every line as hard as frost. The figures in southern landscapes narrow their eyes and maintain a firm jaw. They have seen things that make the dead whimper. But they tough it out.

Auckland is denied any of these foundation myths. Auckland is soft in the middle, not used to the cold. It rollerblades on Tamaki Drive, admires the way sunlight falls through its new curtains, dines al fresco on bok choy and onion bhaji finished with a tamarind and kaffir lime glaze. One of the most famous dates in Auckland's history is July 27, 1939, the day the city witnessed its only recorded snowfall.

Auckland pities Wellington – the wind, the proximity to Masterton – and visits the South Island only to put on a pair of skis. C.K. Stead might pen a line about a heron in flight, then turn in for an early night. Auckland's poetic impulse is wan, overcome by the fructifying heat of summer. In winter, Auckland is overcome by rain. New Zealand's biggest city is New Zealand's only monsoon city, 1.4 million people clinging to a raft, desperate for a sighting of dry land.

A city built on an isthmus – even the word is sticky. A narrow city, built on the strip on the back of a Post-it Note. A bit of rain never hurt anyone, but a lot of rain can hurt everyone packed inside a sticky isthmus; there is a distinct possibility that over one million people are building up various assorted irrational and abiding hatreds.

Television weather presenters move up the map and leave Auckland's forecast until last. Nearly a third of the country's population waits for that cliffhanger, and there it is: the same icons of arrowed rain and black clouds that appeared on the screen the night before, and the night before that. At least you know what to expect: the drains foaming at the mouth; the backyards turning to glue; the dreary domestic detail of washing hung out on the line day after waterlogged day. School janitors have the task of Sisyphus. The low moan in every office: 'It looks like rain.' Followed by the inevitable lower moan: 'It's raining.'

Nothing about this is exclusive to Auckland. It's bad everywhere. Other parts of New Zealand have it worse. You can measure rainfall, but how do you measure the weight of over one million people soaked to the bone?

All that shivering and ah-chooing flesh, all that dampened

and demented spirit. A city swishing its windscreen wipers, wiping its feet on the map, staring out of kitchen windows at a remorseless sky. South is rock and ravine, beech and birch; Auckland in winter is without landscape. It's just figures, over one million of them, trapped inside.

The outdoors exists in memory. Warm, lush Auckland, where you can stick more or less anything in the dirt and it will grow. A tube of concrete sprouted into the Sky Tower. Elsewhere the ground is thick with flame trees and fruit trees, flax and Moreton Bay figs, gnawed at by swarms of cicadas and wild flocks of sulphur-crested cockatoos. But the true heart of Auckland beats underground, in its dank, netherworld network of swamps.

Swamps are the bottom line. Visitors to Auckland are shown the sparkling Waitemata and are told about its other harbour, the Manukau, but residents pick their way around mangroves and mangrove creeks. Mangrovia, slithering and oozing, drags its muddied feet across Auckland's carpet. It's where junk goes to die. Generations of Aucklanders have thrown out washing machines, fridges, shopping trolleys, bicycles, and anything else not tied down by sentiment, into mangroves. And then the rains come, and the creeks overflow, and the washing machines, fridges etc are resurrected, sucked out of the mud and spilled out among all the other debris in this tropical dump.

Things fall apart. Auckland loses its appetite even for tamarind and kaffir lime glaze. The paint peels, the fences sag, the roofs leak. Peeling and shredded, rotten to the core, Auckland in winter can very easily inspire a vision of the city sinking into the swamp. Back to where it came from, straight to hell in a gradual retreat, defeated by the weight of over one million people soaked to the bone.

Spring is in the air. The city will dry out, get back on its feet. A strong tide will clutch back the washing machines, fridges etc. But some things stay buried. Auckland's swamps will receive the ruined finance companies and the destroyed reputations, unable to stay afloat on the raft, washed away by the rain. Old Testament city, raining for 40 days and 40 nights. 41 days and 41 nights. 42 days and 42 nights. 43...

[September 7, 2008]

Richard Clayderman

The cunning old dears who run the hospice op shop in my local shopping plaza know how to draw a crowd. They routinely place the most prized exhibits of their new stock in the front window. Last week it was an album by Richard Clayderman.

It was a bitterly cold day and I had a bad dose of the flu. I felt underwater, closed until further notice, nailed shut. I wanted to sleep for a million years and wake up with the sun on my face. I wanted an end to the suffering of all mankind, but especially my own. I could settle for an album by Richard Clayderman.

Its appearance in the front window of the hospice op shop flickered like the light from a candle. There was such a goodness about it. I was struck by the thought that a great many people in the world had found comfort, possibly a cure for their ills, in an album by Richard Clayderman.

It was called *Dreams*. I liked that. It cost a dollar. I liked that too. I parted with my money and turned to leave when a customer blocked my way to the door and said, 'Would you mind if I had a look at that?' I sized her up. She was a nice old dear wearing a teal cardigan and tartan trousers. Reluctantly,

I handed over my album by Richard Clayderman.

She said, 'You know, I was just talking about him yesterday.'

I said, 'You were talking about Richard Clayderman?'

'Yes.'

'I've never known anyone who's talked about Richard Clayderman.'

'Oh, but he's very popular.'

This was undeniable. He has sold an estimated 90 million albums. He has recorded an estimated 90 million albums. Perhaps I am exaggerating that last figure, but K and Y are the only two letters missing in the A-Z of his discography – titles range from *Antique Pianos* to *Zodiacal Symphony*. Is there anyone who has a complete set of albums by Richard Clayderman?

The old dear said, 'Where do you think he's from? Because that's what me and my friend were talking about. She thought he might be French. I think he's Austrian.'

I said, 'I've always suspected he was a Dutchman.'

'A Dutchman?'

'They're a pretty smooth mob, those Dutch.'

'They are that.'

In fact, he was born Philippe Pages, in Paris. He changed his name when he launched his amazing career in 1976. His breakthrough hit was 'Ballad pour Adeline'. Clayderman has said his worst fear is appearing on stage and not being able to remember how to play. This is surprising – in the past thirty years, he has performed 'Ballad pour Adeline' more than eight thousand times. This month, he has performed it at concerts in Israel, Brazil, Chile and India. He told an interviewer, 'I pay lots of taxes to the French authorities because they are always extremely greedy. I also bought different houses, but it was not a good deal because I always spent a lot on buying them yet sold them for a low price. I have to work a lot now.' But he is always guaranteed good sales in Japan, Hong Kong and China, which are the world's biggest consumers of albums by Richard Clayderman.

The old dear studied his face on the cover of *Dreams*. He has said, 'Sometimes I wish I could be anonymous in order not to be approached by people who want to talk with me or get an autograph but that is part of being Richard Clayderman.' He posed on the album cover with his mouth open, and lowered eyelids. He looked slightly dim. She said, 'He looks like an Austrian Jew to me.' And then she handed me back my copy of the album by Richard Clayderman.

I walked home with it in the rain. I played it all day. It invaded the room like a conquering army; its weapon was syrup, which it threw all over the walls, soaking the carpet, blocking the drains. I got a splitting headache and lay down. But I changed *Dreams* from side one to two, and back again, and again and again, until I felt well enough to do the housework. I laboured for hours, alone and sneezing, my only friend in the world an album by Richard Clayderman.

I began to understand what ninety million people have

understood. I separated the syrup and found a sincerity. He was gentle with Liszt, Mancini, Offenbach; his version of 'Moonlight Sonata' was sensitive; his limpid touch floated 'Für Elise' and 'Love Story' on air. He once said, 'I am rather shy and reserved. I don't speak loud and rarely get irritated. I keep everything inside.' *Dreams* was music from another room, another world, offering hope and warmth. I felt better. Strength returned to the weak flesh and the defeated spirit. By nightfall I thought: never again do I want to listen to an album, any album, by Richard Clayderman.

[September 21, 2008]

A Social Report on Lawn Mowing in New Zealand

We're driving slowly through the neighbourhood and she says, 'Why are you sighing?'

'Because of the verges.'

'The what?'

'The verges. You know. The verges of grass on the sidewalk.'

'Oh. That again.'

'Look! There's another one.'

She doesn't look. She keeps on driving. The car is filled with music: Alanis Morissette on the stereo, while our daughter sits in the back seat and presses tunes on her toy telephone. We're returning from a picnic at the beach. It's a lovely summer evening. But the verges spoil everything.

'I just can't get my head around it. People must really hate each other.'

She says, 'It might not be like that.'

'No, it is like that. It's pure hate. And meanness. Bitter, petty, nasty, sour, churlish, hateful meanness.'

I continue to glare out the window, and feed my rage by detecting yet another unfinished verge. And another one, and another one. They're so easy to notice at this time of year, at the height of grassy summer.

'It's a modern phenomenon. A sign.'

She says, 'A sign of what?'

'A sign of social disease.'

It all started two years ago when workmen began ripping up the sidewalks. They worked slowly and steadily, inch by inch, with their jackhammers and their concrete mixers and their plumb lines. They did a good job. The sidewalks were worn and cracked, and needed repaving. But the road to hell is repaved with good intentions.

The men also tore out the grass verge strip in front of houses. I didn't understand why they did that. And I didn't pay close attention to how they went about it. It's only now that I realise they were sponsoring a silent war.

All I noticed at the time was the sudden brilliant presence of yellowhammers. The birds were attracted by grass seed that workmen had tipped on the exposed soil of the verges. It's hardly an uncommon bird; since it was shipped from England to Nelson, New Zealand, in 1862 it has colonised both islands in great numbers, although anecdotal evidence suggests the population is declining. But I seldom see yellowhammers in my neck of the woods. Small, active, vivid, they swooped on the seed in flocks of about three hundred, and stayed for about two or three weeks, their yellow bodies raining down all day long.

The birds left; the grass grew. It was the beginning of the end of any pretence of good manners and mutual respect. After the grass had settled in, I dragged out the motor mower. It was only then that I realised the verge now stretched across two properties; the workmen had taken out the concrete strip that separated my house and my neighbour's house, and grassed it over. It soon became evident they had practised this strange subversion throughout the neighbourhood.

The fact that neighbours are now forced to share their verge of sidewalk grass has posed an ethical dilemma, and the response has been spiteful. Half of almost every elongated verge is neatly mowed, while the other half remains hairy, wild, neglected, snubbed.

The entire neighbourhood is marked by these lines drawn in the grass. It's a bizarre and faintly depressing sight. Something rotten has been exposed. It takes only a few minutes to mow the remaining half of a verge: why not lend a helping hand? What's wrong with people?

She says, 'You're actually seething. Stop it. It's making Fatty tense.'

'Fatty's all right. Anyway, she should be made aware of what's going on. It's a valuable childhood lesson.'

'Look, it could be that people feel they'd be trespassing by mowing their neighbour's half of the verge. Or that they don't want to impose.'

'What?'

'They might be being sensitive. They might think it is rude to mow someone else's verge.'

'No. It's selfish, it's lazy, it's immoral. It's a lack of kindness. It's the absence of a generosity of spirit. It's clear evidence of hate.'

Maybe it's an Auckland thing but I doubt it. Beware the day workmen arrive on your street and rip up the sidewalks. Beware the day of the yellowhammer.

We get home. The grass verge in front of our house and the neighbour's house is immaculate.

She says, 'You think you're the last virtuous man in New Zealand.'

'No, I don't.' We both know I'm lying.

[January 25, 2009]

End Days

A metaphor for the global economic crisis arrived on my street at 1.24 a.m. last Thursday. I couldn't sleep; it was one of those humid summer evenings in Auckland when oxygen is evicted from the air, the house wilts like a flower, and the silence is so epic that you could, if you set your mind to it, hear the dripping of a tap in a house in Bluff. But it was another, closer noise which got me out of bed at 1.24 a.m.

It was the sound of the engine of a truck in first gear. It was growling towards my house. I pulled back the curtain, and peeped through the venetian blind. All I could see through the leaves of the persimmon tree in the front garden was a flashing orange light. It twirled in the darkness. Police? Ambulance?

I announced, 'I'd better go outside and see what's happening.' She didn't look up from the pages of her paperback book. She was reading *Anna Karenina*. Outside, a possible matter of life and death, inside, an early chapter of a masterpiece by a Russian genius, and the best she could say was, 'Yeah, yeah.'

I opened the door and stepped on to the porch. I saw what was happening. I walked back into the bedroom and said,

'Come and have a look.' I love it when she runs through the house. She has long lovely legs and her feet barely seem to touch the floor – she bounds like some elegant creature of the open plains, a new species of fawn, long-haired and adolescent, full of zest and irrepressible good spirits.

She raced to the door and saw what was happening. We both laughed. And then she slipped back to bed and Russia, and I stayed on the porch, with the orange light twirling in the darkness, and watched a large house slowly move down the street like a ship navigating its way through shallows.

It was on the back of a truck. It took up the whole width of the street. Its roof twitched the overhead power lines. There were men on the pavement speaking into walkie-talkies, traffic cones at the end of the street, and a sign reading: WIDE LOAD FOLLOWS.

At first I thought it might be the house due to take its advertised place on a nearby vacant lot. 'Replica villa with wonderful indoor/outdoor flow. Stunning traditional exterior with authentic detailing, but with the benefits of modern, low-maintenance materials.' An artist's impression of the villa shows a woman in a white dress standing on an upstairs balcony and gazing into space. She looks as though she is waiting for death. It will come more quickly than the sale of the house: its asking price is $975,000.

But the villa with wonderful indoor/outdoor flow on the back of a truck had gone past the empty section. To the sneeze of the truck's hydraulics, it was now undulating beneath the power lines, then creaking forward at a rate of knot. I padded to the kitchen, returned with a cup of tea, and continued staring at the spectacle of a WIDE LOAD hogging the road. I thought: where had it come from? And: where was it going? Also: who was inside?

All this summer I have been looking for omens and portents of imminent economic collapse and apocalypse. Every age has its anxiety – nuclear holocaust, plague, terrorism – and right now financial ruin is at the front of the pack. Living through the recession is like waiting for war, or a storm to hit; newspaper headlines about redundancies and another business going to the wall bring it closer, but I have grown impatient for visible signs of disaster, and chaos, and end days. The house brought it home.

Its doors and windows were boarded up. No one, I figured, as I stood sleepless and breathless on the front porch on a humid summer's evening, would be able to hear the occupants calling for help. Poor devils! Trapped inside were a family who had lost their jobs and were in no position to pay the mortgage. The bank foreclosed. Their villa was listed as a mortgagee sale. But the bank already had its hands full trying to flog off thousands of other worthless shacks. What to do? It had called in the government, which inherited the debt, and then swung into action by carting the villa away in the dead of night – along with the family.

Where to? I gave the matter deep thought in the glow of twirling orange light. When I considered the government's recent decision to send young offenders to boot camp, it struck me there could be only one likely destination. The family were en route to Waiouru, a kind of leper colony marooned in the desolate soils of the Rangipo Desert. They would be conscripted into the army, re-educated on subjects of wasteful expenses and social responsibility, given a shovel. They would pay for their house by the sweat of their backs. They would learn their lesson.

She called out, 'What are you doing out there? Come back to bed.' Inside, loved ones, the furniture of home, unpaid bills; outside, an ark tugged out to sea, and the floodwaters rising.

[March 15, 2009]

Missing Person's Report

As a good citizen, I had every intention of making an attempt to return the stack of about twenty business cards I found scattered on the grass in Albert Park in downtown Auckland the other night. I was taking an evening stroll. It was around one a.m. I had run out of cigarettes. A lot of downtown convenience stores stay open late, or never close. One is actually called Dairy. Its name seems quaint, almost ironic. The rest are called Lucky Mart, Happy Mart, Smiley Mart, Star Mart, Pearl Mart, Big Mart, Metro Mart, City Mart, Xpress Mart, Mini Mart, Just Mart – the language of Asia.

I pocketed the cards and kept walking. It's probably not a great idea to saunter around the park at that time of night. But my step is light and quick; all I've ever seen moving was a possum, and all I've ever heard stirring are the homeless men who sleep in the doorways of buildings backing on to the park. Most of the homeless are tangata whenua, people of the land in a green belt with Moreton Bay fig trees, mynahs, blackbirds, starlings, and statues of Governor Grey and Queen Victoria.

There was a young Chinese guy smoking on the front step

of a Mart. Sorry, he said, and then he stood up and walked behind the counter. I asked, How's your night going? He said, There was a fight across the road about thirty minutes ago. I asked what sort of fight. He said five white guys gave the fingers to a passing car. It braked and four Pacific Islander guys jumped out. One man lay on the sidewalk and wasn't moving. An ambulance arrived. Crikey, I said. Crazy, he said.

Back in my apartment, I spread out the cards and looked for clues. There were a lot of names, but none that belonged to whoever had lost the stack. All I could establish was that the owner was probably a female student from Japan who lived on Auckland's North Shore.

A card for Debra Spinetto, programme information adviser with the faculty of health and environmental sciences at the North Shore campus of AUT. A card for Rachel Nordmeyer, banking adviser with the BNZ in Takapuna. A card for Deborah Anne Longhurst, residential sales agent with Barfoot & Thompson in Beach Haven. Loyalty cards for two cafés in Browns Bay. A card for the Bream Bay Butchery ('Meat you can eat!') in Ruakaka, and a card for Family Planning – an appointment had been made for twelve noon in November last year.

The rest of the cards were in various combinations of English and Japanese. A card for Kazumi Teru, passenger baggage handler at Haneda Airport in Tokyo. Two cards for radio station Osaka 851FM. A card for a recording studio called Mahana somewhere in Japan. More cards connected with music: two employees, Michiharu Sato and a character called Seiji 'Ignite' Fukagawa, with Tokyo-based record company Avex. I looked up the company's website. It included a boring message from CEO Masato Matsuura: 'Structural reforms ... consolidating management resources ... current difficulties ... We have commenced development of a new blueprint for achieving hits after having implemented a fundamental review of our business models, governance system, branding strategies and so on for our music business in Asia.'

Another card was for one of Avex's pop stars, Zoey Yuko, although she doesn't seem to have enjoyed much success since recording the dance release 'Soakin' Wet' with US producers Jimmy Jam and Terry Lewis in 2004. YouTube has her debut single – a cover version of Bjork's 'Venus as a Boy'. It's quite fetching. She sings it in Japanese. In the video, she sits on a washing machine in a sparkly red miniskirt, and her bum vibrates.

The paper trail of the cards led nowhere specific. Someone with a bank account, and interests in real estate and pop music; a coffee drinker and a meat eater; a student; Japanese. Yes, that really narrows it down in Auckland. After dark, on weeknights, downtown Auckland is like a shabby deserted province of somewhere in Asia. A lot of students from China, Korea and Japan, a lot of sushi bars and gaming rooms, but hardly any noise, only a few cars on Queen Street, six tired faces — white, brown — on a bus rumbling east, west or south. English is a rare overheard language. The laundry neatly pegged out on the balconies of apartments, the tidy, tightly packed shelves of convenience marts — there are times when you remember National MP Lockwood Smith's disgraceful remark about 'little Asian hands'.

'It may be that this tendency towards generalisation,' drones Asia New Zealand Foundation research director Dr Andrew Barber in a paper presented in 2007, 'means New Zealand is missing an opportunity to develop cross-cultural communication skills through in-depth interactions with international students.' The students should be viewed as 'essential participants in a national conversation about New Zealand's identity.'

But what about the identity of the owner of the missing cards? Strange to think of that 'essential participant', a fee-paying student one day, chatting to the possibly legendary Seiji 'Ignite' Fukagawa in Tokyo, the next day a new New Zealander, maybe passing through, maybe here to stay, walking in Albert Park. Her white cards looked like small lit windows in the dark.

[June 14, 2009]

Birdland

Porridge is on the breakfast menu every day at our house. The two girls walk into the kitchen, and stop in their slippered feet at the stove. My daughter asks, 'Is that for us?' I look down at her hungry upturned face. Her mother asks, 'Can we have some too?' They have the same trembling mouth. I stir the pot. I consider their appeals. The porridge smells good, fills the kitchen with warmth. It comes to the boil. I allow it to simmer. Reluctantly, with a heavy sigh, I measure a few precious spoonfuls into two bowls, and shoo the girls out. Other customers are waiting. Their need is great. It could be a matter of life or death. I am God. And then I reach for the raisins, the old bananas, the malt and the lard. I am ready to paint my masterpiece.

Oats and animal fat gobbed with fruit and drenched in thick dark malt really is something to behold, and it's even better to eat. As soon as it cools I paddle out into the backyard in my gumboots, climb a stepladder, and dump a plate of the stuff on to a not very flat board which I nailed not very evenly to the top of a pole. Within seconds, and all throughout the day, it attracts mobs of mynahs, starlings, sparrows and silvereyes – birdland, loud and desperate, in rain and wind, throwing their weight around like scraps of wet paper.

The dish is improvised, a work of daring and original genius, possibly, but it owes every debt to one of New Zealand's greatest cookbooks. Published in 2007, Rosemary Tully's *Tea for the Tui: Fun recipes to entice birds to your garden* is a modern classic. Every household ought to have a copy. It's in my household between the *Edmonds Cookery Book* and Ainsley Harriott's *Big Cook Out*.

In 1991, Rosemary launched Whakatane Bird Rescue. Success stories include saving tui suffering from rhododendron poisoning, and a native falcon trapped inside a Pizza Hut. (Bird Rescue Christchurch has dealt with a duck impaled on a TV aerial, and another duck which a thirteen-year-old boy in Laura Kent Place had actually tried to hang with a noose from a tree.) Kiwi, weka, moreporks and numerous other birds have also survived injury and misfortune thanks to Rosemary's efforts. Her book serves the same purpose.

Prepared food is essential for garden birds, especially in winter. It can be as simple as throwing bread on to the garden, or stocking a bird feeder with commercially available wild bird seed. Lower Hutt firm Vitapet sells 500 gram packets for $2.69; very recently, Home Brand has moved into the market and produces two-kilogram bags for $5.99. Home Brand! Strange to think of its best minds gathering in some probably boring room and discussing the capital value of wild birds.

An even cheaper option is sugar stirred inside a jar of water. Tui and silvereyes love it. But how to go about building a high platform that secures the jar, and allows ease of access to refill it? I was stumped, incapable, miserable. I needed help. Help arrived. Radio Live presenter Graeme Hill, widely regarded as the nicest guy in broadcasting, turned up at my door with a pole over his shoulder. Working with an electric drill, a saw and strips of velcro, and wedging the jar in between a circle of upturned nails, he knocked up a detachable feeder in no time flat. It looks like a mast. My backyard is an ocean – birdland, perched and slurping, in high seas, viewed from the kitchen, where I slave over porridge, malt, lard.

The ingredients are listed among the forty or so recipes in *Tea for the Tui* – along with eggs, flour, baking powder, cheese, kidney and haricot beans, split peas, rice, pasta, lentils, millet, sunflower seeds, cornbread, black treacle, unsalted peanut butter, popcorn, kumara, carrots, broccoli, blueberries, vanilla Complan... The meals are easy to make, although Rosemary's instructions for bread pudding requires a steady hand to position cream crackers as a series of steps inside a hollowed-out loaf.

I suspect Rosemary is an Elvis fan. Her recipe for The King's Bread Pudding is 'named in tribute to the similarly fearsome snack of choice that The King enjoyed so much in his later years'. Other recipes include pancake treats, rock cakes, oatcakes, bean soup, breakfast bagels and other dishes that can be either dumped on to the bird table, skewered, wrapped in string bags, or hooked on to lengths of wire mesh.

Brilliant, easy, rewarding. It's true that I ought to go the whole hog and plant various native trees, or cast my eyes beyond the garden and volunteer to help save threatened species. The entire population of fairy terns, New Zealand's rarest endemic bird, is only about forty; disgracefully, the government refuses to fund a warden to look after the birds at their Waipu breeding site this coming summer. Lazily, selfishly, I'll remain in the kitchen, up to my elbows in chocolate malt and animal fat, and keep my eye on birdland — the seven shy, soft Malay spotted doves pecking at the wild bird seed that scatters on to the grass, the tui, silvereyes, mynahs, starlings, sparrows, thrushes and blackbirds falling from the sky. They come to eat and drink. They are very good customers. They always bring a gift.

[July 26, 2009]

The Second Worst Movie Ever Made

Studies show that the worst movie ever made is *Australia*, the expensive Hollywood flop that curled up and died on cinema screens in the summer holidays. I didn't have the strength to see it. The trailer near killed me. Nicole Kidman under a parasol; Hugh Jackman under a beard. TWO PEOPLE FROM DIFFERENT WORLDS. He: 'Welcome to Australia.' She: 'You brute!' Gum trees, Ayers Rock, pet Aborigines. THEIR LOVE DEFIED DESTINY. Nicole Kidman under Hugh Jackman. They run cattle. And then bad people from Japan — the film is set in 1942 — bomb Darwin. She: 'You can't let them win!' He: 'We won't.' Cattle: 'Moo!'

It came out this weekend on DVD. I rented it on Friday night. My eyes were glued to the screen. I watched a modern masterpiece. It was epic, romantic, visually stunning, although occasionally slow-moving. Kidman has never turned in a more subtle performance, and neither has Jackman's beard.

But I didn't actually bother watching *Australia*. I watched the bonus special feature that came with the DVD. Like the main feature, it's over two hours long, is directed by Baz

Luhrmann, and represents a daring Australian vision of a land and its people. He has called it *New Zealand*.

Opening scene: Kidman arrives at Auckland aerodrome on a summer's day in 1942. She waits at the taxi rank and inspects her new country. She gapes at what she sees: sheep, six yokels in rags, Mount Ruapehu. It's raining. It still is by the time a taxi arrives in 1957. Jackman plays the driver. Kidman waits for him to help her with her luggage. She waits until 1963.

He: 'Old bag.'

She: 'How rude!'

He: 'I meant your suitcase. Climb in. Where to?'

She: 'Central Otago.'

He: 'Have you there in no time.'

Scene two: Jackman and Kidman drive through Rotorua on a summer's day in 1971. It's raining. She is distressed by what she sees: steaming mud, wild pigs, Mount Ruapehu.

She: 'What's that?'

He: 'What?'

She: 'That. Standing in front of the WINZ office.'

He: 'Oh, him. That's what we call a Marry.'

She: 'The people of the land.'

He: 'I don't know about that. They keep out of my way and I keep out of theirs. It's just the way it is.'

She: 'Your attitude is ridiculous. The two races must live together in harmony and mutual self-respect before we can claim a national identity.'

He: 'Listen, you've been here five bloody minutes, and –'

She: 'Please hurry. I want to meet more Marries.'

Scene three: Jackman and Kidman drive through the Desert Road. It's the winter of 1984. Frozen lakes, ancient forest, Mount Cook. She bakes scones, and gulps down a bottle of Valium. Lightning forks the brooding sky. Wild horses canter across the road, and so do hobbits.

He: 'About the Marries. Listen, you've been here five bloody minutes, and – '

She: 'Ssshhh. Just hold me.'

He: 'What about Curly?'

She: 'Curly won't mind.'

He: 'Okay. I'll try anything once.'

Scene four: Jackman and Kidman are married the next day in Christchurch by a wise and kindly Māori priest, played by Sam Neill. Curly is the best man. He raises his glass to make a toast, but is too drunk and falls over. Jackman weeps quietly. Kidman bakes a pavlova and announces she is pregnant. Jackman weeps loudly.

She: 'Let's go home.'

He: 'Fair enough. The meter's still running.'

Scene five: Jackman and Kidman arrive at Kidman's high-country station in Central Otago on a summer's day in 1997. It's sunny. They complain. They clear gorse. They complain. They run sheep. They complain. They ride horses. They complain. They raise chickens. The years pass quickly. They walk into town in 2003 and arrive in 2009.

She: 'What's that?'

He: 'What?'

She: 'That. Standing in front of the bank.'

He: 'Oh, him. That's what we call an Australian. Owns the bank. Owns all the banks. Owns mostly everything.'

She: 'We can't let them win!'

He: 'We won't.'

Closing scene: Jackman and Kidman arrive at a busy international airport. They marvel at what they see: clean clothes, good wages, optimism.

He: 'Welcome to Australia.'

She: 'You wonderful man!'

Curly: 'Baaa!'

[April 26, 2009]

The Third Worst Movie Ever Made

Quite possibly the strangest New Zealand film of all time showed up recently on the Sky movie channel TCM. The network buried *Green Dolphin Street* on a Monday afternoon. That was a shame. It deserved a wider audience. It was completely mad.

It was also the first true Hollywood production ever set in New Zealand. A big-budget epic filmed in 1947 and weighing in at 146 minutes, it starred the legendary Lana Turner as a tragic heroine and the not especially legendary Hawai'ian actor Al Kikume (his other film credits include *Bela Lugosi Meets A Brooklyn Gorilla*) as 'A Māori'. Other Māori were played by Mexicans, American Indians, and English actor Patrick Aherne in blackface.

A huge fuss was made about the film even before it was conceived. MGM held a literary competition and announced that the best book would be turned into a film. It received ninety-nine manuscripts. The winner was English novelist Elizabeth Goudge. It made her rich, but she continued to live with her invalid mother; they rest in their family grave among the bluebells and yews at the St Mary Magdalene church cemetery in Hampshire.

The gentle Miss Goudge never visited New Zealand. But her imagination travelled the tyrannies of distance and time. She set her novel in the New Zealand Wars. In the film, a crowd gathers to study a newspaper billboard: NATIVES BURN VILLAGE NEAR AUCKLAND. Aha – Kororareka, 1845. When the heroine is woken by Māori attacking her home, she tells her maid, Hinemoa: 'Hand me my corsets!'

Hinemoa also works as a nanny. 'Take baby,' the heroine commands. 'The noise she makes is not good for the tympanum of my ears.' Her sensitive tympanum is further offended by a haka. You expect rampant cultural insensitivity in *Green Dolphin Street* and you get plenty of that; wood carvings have to be seen to be disbelieved. Also, the New Zealand bush is played by redwood forests in Oregon. Like the author, MGM never visited New Zealand. But the curious thing is that the haka – 'Ka Mate, Ka Mate!' – is for real. I spoke with Wellington film historian David Lascelles and he explained that the National Film Unit provided MGM with authentic audio of New Zealand birds and Māori song.

Lascelles also mentioned that a huge fuss was made about *Green Dolphin Street* during filming – by the New Zealand government. Our man in Washington, George Bennett, approached MGM with an offer to serve as an adviser. They threw him out. 'Can you imagine,' the studio told him, 'Lana Turner learning Māori?'

Well, you expect Hollywood arrogance. And yet Goudge – and the film – display unexpected attention to detail. The accuracy in *Green Dolphin Street* is more shocking than its inventions.

Turner's character first hears about New Zealand from the captain of a trading ship. He gives her a lovely pair of jade earrings, and claims: 'The stone is called tangiwai.' And then he launches into a fine speech. 'New Zealand's a beautiful country. Birds bigger than an ostrich but not able to fly for reason of the heavy stomachs they have on them.' Aha – moa, circa 1400. 'Yes, New Zealand's a grand country,' continues the old fantasist. 'Giant ferns. Ferns that reach above your shoulders! Virgin soil, with timber and flax, and wonderful pastureland, and it don't belong to no one...'

He presents his ravings as facts, but Turner soon learns the truth. She comes to New Zealand in unusual circumstances. Turner's character, Marianne, has a sister, Marguerite. Both fall in love with William. He falls in love with Marguerite but emigrates to New Zealand from the Channel Islands – a great many Channel Islanders emigrated to New Zealand in the nineteenth century. William arrives in Wellington. More realism: it looks extremely boring. He finds the nearest saloon. He writes a letter proposing marriage. But demon rum clouds his mind, and by mistake he addresses it to... Marianne.

'A slip of the pen,' William confesses. But too late. An elated Marianne sails out, marries William, manages his kauri logging business, and gives birth in unusual circum-stances – during a massive earthquake. Geysers bubble and spurt, kauri topple like redwood.

The birth of the new colony is even more troubled. Marianne provides a political analysis. 'The natives who sold land to settlers are killing the Māoris who didn't want to sell.'

Again, Goudge reveals it as nonsense. Glib, domineering, ambitious, Marianne makes a fortune in the Northland kauri trade and then instructs William to buy a sheep station in the South Island. Scots settlers — I can totally believe this — give his money a rapturous welcome. They raise a toast and declare: 'You are the most popular man in Dunedin!' William just wishes he was with his beloved Marguerite, but she mends her broken heart by entering a convent.

Green Dolphin Street won an Oscar for best special effects; the novel became a best-seller. I asked Auckland Central City Library if it had a copy. Yes, in the basement. It deserves to be hauled out, perhaps given a serialised reading on Radio New Zealand. And the film deserves to be screened on TV One, perhaps over two Sunday evenings at prime time. We're so earnest and so cute at telling our own stories; it's more entertaining when someone else tells them.

[August 30, 2009]

A Bird in Takanini

Gwenda Pulham was the first birder I phoned to see about getting a lift out to Takinini so I could twitch the Franklin's gull, but I knew she usually has her hands full. She said she had her hands full. She needed to direct a lawn-mowing man to avoid cutting near the nests of endangered New Zealand dotterels in a grass verge beside the Albany Megacentre.

Next I called Jeremy Wells, the presenter of the TV One series *Birdland*, and he said, 'Yes, love to, where's Takinini?'

The bird had no idea either. It should have been in Peru or Chile on its annual migration, but it switched its flight to Auckland last month, and set off the most popular twitch in New Zealand's birding history. A twitch is the pursuit of a rare bird. A rare bird, in New Zealand, is a vagrant. A vagrant is a bird which has flown off course, by itself, separated, lost, tense, probably doomed, very often from Australia, but the Franklin's gull breeds in Canada, and also in Montana, Dakota and Minnesota. In America it's sometimes called a prairie dove.

The first record of a Franklin's gull in New Zealand was in 2002 in Dunedin, at the Tomahawk Lagoon. Maybe the sign reminded it of home. It stayed for only two days. But on Saturday, September 5 this year, a Franklin's gull was seen by South Auckland birders Tony Habraken and Ian Southey at Kidd's Beach on Manukau Harbour. The twitching sensation of 2009 started then and there.

I ran into Tony at the launch of Keith Woodley's book, *Godwits: Long-haul Champions*. The famous author was busy signing copies of his book, but in my awe of the Franklin's gull I regarded Tony as the celebrity. I rushed to his side, shared breathing space with the man who discovered a miracle. He said he'd heard the gull before he saw it. Hello, he thought, and took a close look. It had a black head, like a hood. Its back was dark grey, and its primary feathers seemed worn. It flew away.

Word went around that night on the email discussion group *birding-nz*. Two twitchers charged off to Kidd's the next day. No luck. None the next few days, either. A twitcher wrote on *birding-nz*: 'I have been around the Manukau from Hillsborough to Waiuku. No Franklin's. Exciting and frustrating.' Another man, obviously a dreadful pessimist, claimed the bird had already disappeared, 'done a runner'.

On Friday, September 18, though, Phil Hammond's smart birding detective work led to a sighting of the bird at Ardmore Airfield, feeding on insects by the runway, and later that day it was seen drinking water from a pond at Bruce Pulman Park in Takanini. Both sightings were sent through to *birding-nz*, but not quick enough for an agitated twitcher with the curious user name Optikop: 'What an utter disaster that the finders weren't able to pass this info on until the evening when it was too late!'

Further sightings over the next few days ran hot. 'Best seen from the airfield cafe...' 'Fed with bread by a young family at the pond...' 'Flying back and forth between Ardmore and Takanini...' 'On the pond again...' 'Warming itself on tarseal...' 'Preening on the pond...' 'It landed on a lamp post above our car and we watched it for an hour while happily snacking on biscuits.'

By this stage it already seemed certain that more people around New Zealand had travelled to twitch the Franklin's gull than any other rare bird, beating the record probably held by the Australian reed-warbler at St Anne's Lagoon in Cheviot in 2004. But then all hell broke loose on *birding-nz*. Optikop, perhaps driven to distraction by not being able to find the damned bird, claimed evidence of 'a suppression incident', that news of the Franklin's gull sighting had been 'kept quiet ... withheld'. He wrote: 'I'd have expected local birders would be flying the flag at such an historic event. But no, every visiting birder I met (they came from Northland, Waikato, Bay of Plenty, Hawke's Bay, Wellington, Canterbury, UK and Canada) commented on the eerie total absence of local birders. ... The situation is as unsatisfactory as a bloke who leaves the pub when it's his round.'

This base accusation was met with a riposte from no less an authority than the president of the New Zealand

Ornithological Society, who wrote: 'With all due respect this statement is a load of drivel. To suggest there was a conspiracy of silence is just ludicrous.' But the bad vibes continued. One person wrote: 'Some of the unintentional suppression and apathetic attitude to rarities that I have witnessed here over the past twenty years would take your breath away.' Another responded, 'Why do foreign birders continue whingeing, and making up stories about a covert birding clique?' Then this: 'It would be a shame if birders are put off reporting rarities in case they are subjected to ill-informed personal attacks.'

The bird made no comment. 'There it is,' said Jeremy, as he drove into Bruce Pulman Park on Tuesday, September 29 and pointed to something amazing – the Franklin's gull, a visitor from the Gulf of Mexico which had ended up on the wrong coast of the Pacific, resting on loose gravel beside a scrum machine, solitary, petite, red-billed, moulting, listening to a nearby tui.

[October 11, 2009]

A Postcard from Auckland

Two friends are right now enjoying a holiday on a cruise ship in the Caribbean. Another chum, a successful author, emails from the first week of his fourteen-city book tour of Germany: 'Am writing on a sun-drenched terrace of a hotel in the countryside, surrounded by fat wealthy Bavarians convalescing, it seems, from the rigours of banking.' I turn on TV and there's some old trout hosting *Intrepid Journeys*; she screeches New Zealand syllables at bewildered passers-by somewhere amazing in South America. I go to the library and take out an illustrated book of Paul Theroux's travels – a yak in Tibet, a water buffalo in Burma, a holy dwarf in Madras.

The whole waiting world, with its sights and wonders, its ancient miseries and fabulous unfamiliarities. But travel can be near-flung. Even in our own neighbourhood, we are all strangers in a strange land. A journey can be as simple as the daily hoof up to the shops and back home again. Today I hoofed up the shops and back home again.

Brain-dead dogs howled in damp backyards. Supermarket shopping trolleys lay in creeks, on the roadside, up trees. There were crushed cans of Diesel Bourbon & Cola in the gutters, and a Somalian family delivering junk mail. Four people sat dazed at a bus stop with plastic shopping bags at their feet. They looked as though they had waited a very long time. It was day five of a bus strike.

Outside the supermarket, two Māori women stopped for a chat. 'Are you still living behind the Mad Butcher?' Corned silverside $5.99 a kilo; THE 2 PEOPLE IN THE PHOTO BELOW ARE NOT WELCOME IN THIS STORE. Inside, a raving customer asked for a refund. 'It's for the can of green beans. There's nothing wrong with them. It's just that I don't want them. I don't know why I bought them. I don't like green beans. What am I going to do with green beans?' Twenty-five percent or more off all Wattie's products while offer lasts; metal star Christmas tree topper $4.99.

The first insinuation of Christmas, the first promise of summer revealed by the way sunlight rests against a garden wall. Here, in a sensual corner of the South Seas, the air feels ripe above the nearby reef, and breezes comb the hair of willow trees. Eels spell out the letter S in the creek, white-faced herons build nests in the top of pines. Red bottlebrush needles are about to fall and scatter on the pavement. Accommodation options include a boarding house for the mad.

One of the guests shuffled through the plaza. He wore a pair of tracksuit pants that looked as though they might be swollen with water, like a deep-sea diver's costume. In fact the pants were concealing thick sheepskin rugs wrapped around his legs.

He walked into the covered arcade. There was a beach towel decorated with a picture of Hannah Montana for sale at the $2 Shop, and the whole waiting world lay in a thousand pieces at the hospice op shop. There were jigsaws of sights in San Diego and York, and the scattered muzak of *James Last In Russia* on vinyl. Allah lurked in the shelves of a Middle Eastern grocery, and so did packets of biscuits called Rich & Rich.

But the arcade felt like a tomb. It did its best to stamp out any signs of life. A sign advised: NO SMOKING. NO BICYCLES. NO SKATEBOARDS. NO DOGS. Another sign warned against buskers and beggars: WE WILL EN-FORCE THIS BY CALLING THE POLICE. Was that even legal? The buskers had played outside the arcade. A man approached and asked why I was writing the sign's message in a notebook. He said he managed the arcade. I asked why he had banned buskers. 'There were complaints.' Was he aware of any support for the buskers? 'No.' But this was ignorant and stupid. A lot of passers-by gave money to the buskers. 'It's a free country,' he said. I said you wouldn't think so, not in his mean-spirited and officious arcade. He ran away like a girl.

The community centre warned against visitors who showed signs of swine flu. Its noticeboard included a card from a man wanting a job: I AM LOOKING FOR WORK IN COLD STORE. I HAVE 7 YEARS EXPERIENCE IN COLD STORES. Next to it was a card scrawled with a verse from Psalms: LOOK YE! BEHOLD THE BEARD OF AARON AND SEE THE OIL OF HONEY AND WINE FLOWING DOWN HIS BEARD! But you could behold a similar sight in the plaza, where the town drunk sat with Diesel Bourbon & Cola flowing down his beard. He said, 'I know Graham Brazier. Do you know Graham?'

Here, in an apparently unremarkable Auckland suburb, flat, neatly mowed, swampy, picket-fenced, roaring with dogs, I walk back home – stopping at the service station to buy cigarettes from a Pacific Island woman whose name tag reads REJOYCE, then past the Catholic Legion of Mary centre with a supermarket shopping trolley left on the lawn – and feel the need to put my feet up. All travel is enriching and exhausting. An even more exotic destination awaits next week: Wellington.

[October 25, 2009]

A Postcard from Wellington

Strange to wake up in a town where you used to live. Dawn, damp under low cloud, washed out, tender, dreamy, the light rolling over in its sleep from black to grey, last night's rain gargling in the drains, the kind of classic Wellington morning that you know has set in for the rest of the day, a nothing day, overcast and vaguely bleak, filling in time 'til nightfall, the kind of day that if you lived there you'd wake up to and think was a complete drag.

But from the window of my hotel room it looked gorgeous – underwater, smoky. The hotel was downtown, between The Terrace and Lambton Quay. I got up and walked both streets. The city was pale and deserted. Commuters were yet to stamp through the railway station, grabbing at coffee and *The Dominion Post*. I knew this time of morning well. The first time I lived in Wellington, poor and dishonest, I picked my way along The Terrace and Lambton Quay at dawn, filching milk and bread left outside offices. Milk and bread are still left outside offices. It felt refreshing to swig from a bottle as I mooched in the soft light towards the revolving doors – every three years, you lot in, you lot out – of parliament.

There was the fat-bummed Beehive, and there was the familiar static surrounding it of good intentions, sick minds and powerful vanities. Above, the pine needles on Tinakori Hill, the air fresh and clean; below, the static heading towards the despairing ministries, departments, foundations, authorities, commissions, boards, councils, agencies, trusts, institutes, and other assorted government quangos stuffed inside high-rise towers back along The Terrace and Lambton Quay, and Bowen Street and Featherston Street. The sandwiches in briefcases; the boring pamphlets at reception.

I had spent the previous evening at a function attended by about two hundred public servants from despairing ministries, departments, etc. They were a friendly and amusing bunch, glad of the chance to guzzle a free drink in this age of cutbacks and cost-cutting, and naturally the talk turned to working conditions under the National government. They said their new masters spoke about the big picture, and urgency, and action, but the reality was National's incompetence, bungling, naïveté, recklessness, intellectual sloth, and, inevitably, foul-mouthed tantrums – a particular figure of contempt and loathing was foreign affairs minister Murray McCully.

Wellington politics, Wellington rain. It poured down hard that night. The best place to see it was on the waterfront. I was on the waterfront. It drowned the harbour, applauded in your ears. I thought of how much wilder it would sound if for some strange reason you were standing in darkness out on the pier at Petone, the jetty at Days Bay, the beach squirming with kelp at Makara – so much of Wellington clings close to the coast. The last time I lived in Wellington I watched a herd of cattle stampede along the shore at Pencarrow. That same day, I halted my bike when I came across a seal on the track. It woofed, then flopped down to the rocks, into the waves, and swam away. It made it to a downtown wharf for a spot of sunbathing: its photo was on the front page of the paper.

I could only wander around downtown on my flying visit. Underwater, smoky, low cloud muffling all noise, it lay beneath a cone of silence, quiet and still, the harbour flat and smooth, colourless. It felt like the most serene city in the world. Half-seen through mist, it seemed ancient, at least medieval.

But downtown looked spruce, modern. In the second and longest time I lived in Wellington it looked like a bombsite, excitingly shabby. It had an excellent range of tea rooms, and a thousand draughty pubs. There was a sense of abandonment. God knows why. In the forest of the town belt there was an abandoned swimming pool, an abandoned observatory, an abandoned nursing home. I worked in an office beneath an abandoned bowling alley, and took another job in the basement of an abandoned waterfront rotunda. Possibly more relevant to mankind were the film writers who lived rent-free in an abandoned apartment building on Courtenay Place. They later made a movie about hobbits.

THE STATE WE'RE IN

I liked that old Wellington. I liked this new Wellington, or my glimpse of it, as I mooched here and there. As a creature of habit, whenever I return I always walk to Cuba Street and stock up on hot delicatessen food at München Burgers to take home on the flight. I walked to Cuba Street and stocked up on hot delicatessen food at München Burgers to take home on the flight. I was a visitor from out of town in the town where I lived, all up, for twelve years, when I was as harried and grumpy as everyone else on a damp overcast day. The slow hours, the vast parade of umbrellas.

Now, more or less on holiday, a fatter shadow of my former self, in Wellington but not of it, I was dazed by its beauty and tenacity — a weather-beaten island in the harbour, the houses digging their heels into the hillsides, the lovely low cloud reducing the day to a whisper. I had nowhere to go except, happily, leave.

[November 1, 2009]

To Speak to a Customer Services Representative

There was a gunshot, breaking glass, dogs barking. A shout: 'I'm gonna kill both of youse!'

A man's whisper: 'Call the police.'

A woman's whisper: 'You do it.'

Footsteps, the creak of the floor, the reassuring ringtone. It rang once...twice...three times...seven...nine...

He hissed: 'Pick up, pick up!'

On the eighteenth ring, a clear confident voice came on the line, and said, 'Thank you for calling the New Zealand emergency service. If you know the extension of the person you wish to speak to, dial it now, followed by the hash key. Main menu. For personal options, press one.'

The squeak of a pressed keypad.

The voice said, 'For civil defence, press one. For an ambulance, press two. For the fire service, press three. For the police, press—'

A shout: 'Gonna blow your heads off!'

The voice continued, 'To speak to a customer service representative, press five.'

The squeak of a pressed keypad.

The voice said, 'You have reached the ministry of civil

defence. You've called us outside our normal business hours, which are eight a.m. to four p.m. Monday to Friday, and one p.m. to 3.30 p.m. Saturday. For a tsunami, press one. For a terrorist attack—'

The slam of the receiver. Then the reassuring ringtone... A voice said, 'You have reached the police. Your call is important to us. Please continue to hold.'

Bic Runga sang, 'Something good will come my way.'

A voice interrupted the song. It said, 'You can continue to hold, or visit us on dub dub dub dot it's a matter of life and death dot nz forward slash help. That's dub dub—'

The slam of the receiver. Footsteps, the creak of the floor; a woman's whisper: 'When did they say they'll get here?'

A man's whisper: 'I couldn't get through.'

'Try again!'

'I'm going to! But you try on your cell phone, okay?'

'I don't know where it is!'

'I'll ring it.'

'No! He'll hear!'

'I get the feeling he already knows we're here.'

Footsteps, the creak of the floor, the merry tune of the cell phone, playing 'Night Fever' by the Bee Gees.

A shout: 'I heard that!'

The reassuring ringtone. A woman's whisper: 'Pick up, pick up!'

And then a shout: 'I'm gonna burn the house down!'

The squeak of a pressed keypad. A voice said, 'Enter your

four-digit security password followed by the star key. Or to be connected to the fire service for fifty cents and any applicable call charges, press one now. Or hold for a customer services representative.'

A woman's whisper: 'Oh, God.'

Dave Dobbyn sang to her, 'Why are you waiting? Waiting for what?'

A man's whisper: 'Any luck?'

A woman's whisper: 'Not yet. You?'

Bic Runga sang to him, 'I want to hear about your day.'

Dave Dobbyn sang to her, 'I know you're loyal.'

A man's cheerful voice interrupted the song. He said, 'Hello, can I be helping for you, please?'

She whispered, 'Is that the fire service?'

'No, madam, you have be reaching the message service for the constabulary. Can I be taking message, please?'

'You're a cop?'

He laughed, and said, 'No, madam, I am working for call centre in New Delhi.'

'You're not in New Zealand?'

'Oh! It is be my dream to visit your beautiful country, madam.'

She swore at him, and whispered: 'I hung up. This is hopeless.'

A man's whisper: 'I'm on my third song.'

Neil Finn sang to him, 'Don't dream it's over.'

Two short sharp beeps.

A shout: 'I heard that!'

A man's whisper: 'Someone's texted you! See who it is!'

A woman's whisper: 'It says, "Fuck you, madam."'

'Oh, God. Look, I'm hanging up. I'm just going to have to go outside and talk to him, see if I can calm him down.'

Footsteps, a door opening. And then a ringing phone.

She said, 'Hello?'

A clear confident voice said, 'This is a computerised message from Telecom. We don't seem to have received your latest bill payment. If the account is in your name, press...'

There was a gunshot.

[April 18, 2010]

THE NATIONAL STOMACH

Pineapples and Ham

Let us now praise really horrible meals. Really horrible meals were once a permanent fixture on the tables of the nation. They made us gag, squirm, weep, and turn to drink, but they also formed the New Zealand character, shaped the New Zealand identity. This island nation came of age thanks to really horrible meals.

We believed that meat should be served with fruit, especially pineapple. Cheerfully, inevitably, Alison Holst led the way. Let us open her 1976 cookbook *Lamb for All Seasons*. There we will find lamb with pineapple and bacon ('brown pineapple in meat drippings'), lamb kiwifruit curry, lamb and apple casserole, lamb steaks with tamarillos, skillet lamb with pineapple, baked lamb steaks with pineapple, fruity lamb roast, fruity lamb chops, and fruit glazed lamb ('arrange 6–8 pineapple rings along leg').

But we will find stranger dishes. We will find lamb chops in lager, lamb fondue, and lamb with spaghetti: 'Brown 1 kg neck chops on both sides, place in casserole, cover and bake. … Serve meat on spaghetti.'

The pictures do the talking in two books from 1974, *The Australian Women's Weekly Great Chicken Cookbook*, and

The Australian Women's Weekly Great Ways with Steak and Chops. The front cover of the latter shows a big fat lamb chop decorated with crinkle-cut potato chips. The former boasts an incredible photograph of chicken salad in aspic. It looks like a jam roll, except it's chicken and not jam, and possibly not food. 'Surprisingly easy to make ... Serve as one of the dishes for a buffet party.' Then stand well back.

The captions are succinct, insane. 'Veal, lobster and asparagus make an irresistible combination.' The recipe for chicken veronique calls for the chook to be served with green grapes. 'Note: when grapes are out of season, canned grapes can be used.'

Let us turn to two other 1970s' cookbooks found in op shops. Both are heavily stained; someone, somewhere, got busy in a New Zealand kitchen with Johanna Mathie's *Favourite Scottish Recipes* and Caroline Liddell and Nickey Ross's *Ulcer Superdiet: Delicious dishes for sensitive stomachs*. One of the Scottish recipes is for whisky and chocolate crunch. Crush six ounces of chocolate digestive biscuits and place into glass sundae dishes; whip together one pint of cream, three tablespoons of whisky, one ounce of caster sugar, and two drops of vanilla essence; chill, serve, and decorate with grated chocolate. Och, just cut to the chase and drink the rest of the whisky. As for the ulcer cookbook, the recipe for brains with eggs au gratin contains this blithe advice: 'The brains will require the usual soaking and cleaning, then poaching and draining.'

Published in 1985, Tony Simpson's *An Innocent Delight: The Art of Dining in New Zealand* exists as an eccentric and possibly satirical classic. As you read on, you keep thinking: Is this guy serious? Is his book a giant wind-up, a jape, a parody, a con, a have, a hoax, an elaborate black comedy? At any moment, you suspect he will launch into a variation of Swift's famous solution to famine: 'A young healthy child ... will make a delicious and nourishing food, whether stewed, roasted, baked or boiled; and I make no doubt that it will equally serve in a fricassée or a ragoût.'

Let us inspect Simpson's inventions. Hare in chocolate sauce. Cauliflower with wine. Tongue and mushroom crumble. Lamb stuffed with crab. Steaks in black coffee: 'You will need 300 ml of cold, strong, strained black coffee (not instant!). Into this stir a teaspoon of salt, some pepper and the juice of half a lemon and marinate your steaks for about two hours...'

Much of it reads like one man's midlife crisis. Simpson writes in his introduction: 'Some years ago, after a break of well over a decade, I found myself living alone.' No sad bachelor, he; Simpson throws himself into hosting dinner parties, and pursues his dream of 'indoor decadence'. Railing against New Zealand's 'ghastly cult of wholesome food', he pigs out big-time, literally. There is a recipe for pig's ears with lentils ('Wash the ears thoroughly and singe off the bristles') and another for something called pig's head cheese.

'Get the butcher to split the head into two or three parts,

and be sure that you have got the tongue. ... You may find it best to put your pig's head in a brine for a couple of days.' Simpson finds it best. His brine includes water, sea salt, brown sugar and saltpetre. 'You may have a little trouble with the saltpetre as it is one of the principal constituents of gunpowder. You will get a suspicious look at the pharmacy and be asked to sign for it.'

He ends on a note of high lyricism. 'I serve this dish at Easter. Not only is it good for a long weekend but it is a melancholy farewell to summer and autumn. ... Being a valedictory it naturally needs a mustard sauce.'

Amazing. Were you there? Did you survive? And can you claim to have eaten worse than pig's head cheese? Are you the author of a recipe for a really horrible meal? Or, more likely, the victim? Please, send in your recipes, or exhume your repressed memory syndrome for really horrible meals. It's important. One of the great chapters of the New Zealand experience needs to be collected, written, shared. Our stomachs, our selves.

[November 15, 2009]

Bananas and Ham

Waitangi weekend, and the tables of the holiday nation are groaning with food. But once upon a fairly recent time that groan could be heard from the heart, as New Zealanders sat down to eat things that could only loosely qualify as food, and more accurately qualify as a kind of comedy, or calculated insult. For years, our national dish was slop.

In an earlier column I listed just some of the infinite varieties. Readers were asked to raid their repressed memories and send in other examples. They did so in droves. Certain themes emerged – the boiling and saucing of food, and the boiling and saucing of mum's kitchen skills. Angie: 'As a teenager I remember Mum cooking boiled mutton with parsley sauce. There is no recipe. You boil the living daylights out of a leg of mutton, then pour a truly disgusting parsley sauce over it.' Sue of Rotorua: 'Mum used to cut leeks into thin lengths, boil the hell out of them until they separated into strands, then pour a truly disgusting white sauce over it.'

Allison told of a friend's father who lived in a boarding house with other young labourers; the landlady sent the men off with a packed lunch consisting of porridge sandwiches.

Rhys kept a recipe for chicken stuffed with popcorn. Preheat oven to 220 degrees. Brush size 18 chicken with one cup melted butter, and season. Fill cavity with one cup each of stuffing and popcorn. Then: 'Place in baking pan with the neck end toward the front of the oven.' And: 'Listen for the popping sounds.' The punchline: 'When the chicken's bum explodes, the oven door bursts open, and the chicken is hurled across the room, it's done.'

The comedy of other submitted recipes was perhaps more discreet, but try telling that to the pukeko featured in *New Zealand the Beautiful Cookbook* by Tui Flower and Robyn Martin, published in 1993. 'I have whiled away many an afternoon looking through this book,' wrote Hilary. 'It contains such delights as Casserole of Swan and my personal favorite, Pukeko Soup, which calls for one plucked and gutted pukeko, one carrot, one onion etc.'

I was too scared to ask about the 'etc', although I suspect it may have included that ancient New Zealand ingredient, the pineapple. How ancient? Duncan sent a link to a cookbook produced by Wellington's Onslow College, circa 1960. It included Mrs Patrick's recipe for pineapple cheese loaf, and P. Napier's recipe for steak and pineapple: 'Roll blade steak in flour, place pineapple rings on top, sprinkle with brown sugar and a squeeze of lemon juice, and pour over a tin of tomato soup. Bake two hours in casserole.' Onslow alumni include 15,317 vegetarians, 829 maniacs, and a lot of short people.

The recipes serve as a reminder that the first law of great New Zealand slop was to combine meat with fruit. Robin reached for a 1967 recipe book produced by the Wairarapa Red Cross Ladies Auxiliary. It answered the question on everyone's lips: 'How to smarten up old chops.' The solution: place old chops in a roasting dish with plenty of fat, then add a can of apricots. Crush the fruit, and stir with a teaspoon of curry powder. Bake until done, then phone the Red Cross for emergency assistance.

But true madness was achieved in Australia. Kieran pointed to *Be Bold With Bananas*, published circa 1975 by the Australian Banana Growers Council. It features on the website of that superb second-hand bookstore in Wellington, Arty Bees. Let us inspect the contents. Banana sausages. Bananas and ham. Curried meat with banana – choose between chuck steak and chicken. Banana duck with orange sauce. Banana paella. Banana and egg salad. Note: when out of season, canned bananas can be used.

In the spirit of Anzac rivalry, it's to be hoped that someone, somewhere in New Zealand produced something on near or equal footing with Australia's bananarama. The kiwifruit growers council? The feijoa growers council? A lost masterpiece may have come out of the Beef and Lamb Marketing Bureau, those desperadoes who attempt to persuade the nation that New Zealand steak is half-decent. Readers are once again urged to fossick through their shelves or share their haunted memories for evidence of great New Zealand slop.

But it's a fallacy to think of terrible meals as a past sin. There be monsters in the present day. Heidi passed on these tips from a new packet of Sanitarium Weet-Bix: 'Savoury or sweet, Weet-Bix makes a great snack base. Try sliced tomato, drizzled olive oil, a sprinkling of basil or oregano and a twist of black pepper. Another option is Marmite and sliced avocado. Kids will love this one!' Just add pineapple.

[February 7, 2010]

More Kitchen Nightmares

Yes, another celebration of New Zealand's proud history of creating, cooking, and serving slop. The series began with the opening sentence: 'Let us now praise really horrible meals.' Why? Good of you to ask. The answer: 'They made us gag, squirm, weep, and turn to drink, but they also formed the New Zealand character – this island nation came of age thanks to really horrible meals.' Readers provided the next column with many stunning examples of eating, suffering and surviving great New Zealand slop.

Today, more atrocities, more lunacies, more kitchen nightmares; in short, more of the same – you can never have enough of a bad thing, especially when it reveals so much about distinctly New Zealand qualities of ingenuity, naïveté, stupidity, sadism and hate. Hate is a strong word, but a pathological rage seems to underline the 1976 edition of the Women's Division of Federated Farmers' *Recipe Book and Household Guide*, kindly supplied by Theo.

Its hatred isn't directed at people, although the foreword reads like a threat. 'Country brides have always been presented with this book,' writes WDFF president Eleanor C. Watson, 'and through the members of other countrywomen's organisations it has travelled round the world.' The hatred is directed at meat. New Zealand, land of the lamb led to slaughter, the beast swinging on a hook, the roadside signs reading HOME KILLS – is it this long, bloody history of violence that explains the warped minds simmering inside rural kitchens? The recipe book recommends boiled mutton with parsnips and turnips, boiled pork with parsnips and mustard sauce, and grilled steak with pickled walnuts. Country grooms have always trembled at the sight of this book.

Then there are the suggestions beneath the mirthless headline CHEER UP THAT CHOP. They include a thin slice of lemon with a stuffed olive standing in the centre, a spoonful of minced onions mixed with a 'generous pinch' of curry powder, and a paste of hard-boiled egg yolk, seasoning and butter rolled into small balls and placed on the chop, which by that stage is back up on its legs and away laughing, hysterically, out the door.

One man's meat is a federated farmer's wife's poison. The recipe for Spanish Bananas reads thus: 'Slice four ripe sound bananas lengthwise with a silver knife. Chop twelve walnuts. Arrange lettuce leaves on four plates, and place a sliced banana on each. Sprinkle with the nuts. Coat with mayonnaise seasoned with cayenne pepper.' Make an appointment with a Freudian analyst.

Angela, meanwhile, reached for a copy of *Recipe Book and Home Science Notebook*, published by the Wellington Education Board in 1964. It included this scarcely credible recipe for curry: 'Cut into cubes half pound raw beef. Peel and chop finely one onion. Peel and chop one apple and one banana. Melt one tablespoon dripping.

'Fry onion, apple and banana together till brown,' it really does continue, 'and add one teaspoon curry powder. Put in meat and fry 'til brown. Add one dessertspoon coconut and a few raisins, then one cup water and half a teaspoon salt. Simmer gently for one and half hours!' The exclamation mark is probably inserted by Angela, but you never know – the fruit combo browned in dripping may well have driven the author mad with excitement. Finally: 'Thicken with two tablespoons flour, mixed to a smooth paste with cold water.' Oh, and a PS: 'The following may be added to greatly improve the flavour. Coconut, orange segments, orange rind, and pineapple.'

Pineapple. Of course! Research shows it's one of the staple ingredients of great New Zealand slop. When unavailable, try peaches. Louise of Wellington transcribed a recipe ('The worst I've ever read') for Chicken Indienne from *High Fibre Cookbook* by Audrey Ellis, published in 1985. Basically, it called for four chicken pieces cooked in onion, garlic, various spices, and two tablespoons of mango chutney. So far so reasonable. But then: 'Simmer for twenty-five minutes and carefully add four cans of peaches. Cook for five more minutes.'

Follow these further instructions to the letter. Cook wholewheat spaghetti, drain, and toss with French dressing.

'Transfer to a serving dish. Arrange the chicken pieces and peaches on top. Garnish with lemon wedges and parsley sprigs.' Ride a bicycle underwater. Set the alarm for quarter to twenty-nine o'clock. Cook your head, drain, and toss with French dressing.

One final meal, courtesy of Priscilla. It's from the deathless pages of the Selwyn District Girl Guides *300 Favourite Recipes*, published circa 1961. Basically, it calls for homemade sausage rolls baked in a hot oven for an hour with the contents of a large tin of tomato soup. Edible, possibly, if starving to death; but you still have to get past what the dish is actually called. There it is, in big bold letters, on page 17: NIGGER IN THE WOODPILE.

More, please. All ancient and quite insane recipes gratefully received. Together, we are rewriting New Zealand history; together, we are opening up a can of worms, and serving with pickled walnuts.

[March 21, 2010]

HISTORY

Did a Set of Tongs Kill Cook?

February 14 marks another anniversary of the death of Captain Cook. He was killed on that day 230 years ago. The great explorer, who brought the outside world to New Zealand and the South Pacific, was clubbed, stabbed, and drowned on a lovely beach in Hawai'i. The body was dismembered. A few of his remains – including his legs but not his feet, his skull and scalp with one ear missing – were recovered, and buried at sea. He was fifty years old.

Immense scholarship has amounted to a kind of autopsy report: history demands serious analysis of why Cook met such a death. Authors such as Anne Salmond, Glyn Williams, Nicholas Thomas and even Vanessa Collingridge, the best-selling author of a frankly terrible pseudo-biography, are intent on discovering new aspects to a tragedy. But all history is ultimately dragged down to the level of farce. The hopeless comedies of bric-a-brac, trivia and petty finance – the stuff of daily life – played their part in leading Cook to that fatal shore on a summer's morning in 1779.

When I opened up my copy of Salmond's masterful study *The Trial of the Cannibal Dog*, I was surprised to find I had become one of those people who slip newspaper clippings inside their books. It was a story about the auction of the 'spear' that killed Cook. The weapon was bought by an anonymous London woman for 135,000 pounds. Leaving aside its dubious authenticity – Cook was stabbed with an iron dagger – the antique that ought to be more prized is a set of tongs.

The theft of armourer's tongs from the *Discovery* was crucial to Cook's death. A chief had filched them from the ship, was caught, and flogged with forty lashes. If that punishment sent a message, it was ignored by another Hawai'ian, who climbed on board the ship, ran across the deck, grabbed the tongs from under the crew's nose, and then jumped overboard with his bounty. He fled back to the beach at Kealakekua Bay in a canoe. Cook's men took chase. An innocent chief was apprehended, and clobbered over the head with an oar.

The previous harmony enjoyed by crew and islanders – there were feasts, exchanges of gifts, lots of sex – was undone by the incident of the tongs in the daytime. The next day one of the ship's boats, a cutter, was stolen. Cook decided that enough was enough. He was already exasperated by the thieving of his own crew. The price of sex with a Hawai'ian woman was a nail; Cook's men scavenged nails from the inside and outside of the ship.

Three months earlier, when the *Discovery* had anchored at Maui, a cheerful party of Hawai'ians had rowed out to greet the ship. Women gestured to the sailors with 'lascivious motions and gestures'. But Cook wouldn't allow them on board, and refused his men permission to go ashore. To make matters worse, he impounded the crew's grog. All they could drink was a beer brewed from sugar cane. It was, he said, 'very palatable and wholesome'. He had gone too far. The men had put up with walrus meat in the Arctic, but to be deprived of sex and spirits and fobbed off with an alcopop... 'None of my mutinous crew,' Cook complained in his journal, 'would even so much as taste of it.'

Cook's erratic behaviour on his third and final voyage remains a mystery. Wellington's Alexander Turnbull Library commemorated the bicentenary of Cook's death in 1979 by publishing a handsome limited-edition lecture by his biographer and editor of his journals, J.C. Beaglehole. *The Death of Captain Cook* suggests that Cook was 'a tired man' when he left England. 'A hypothesis of some physical cause is hard to resist.' Beaglehole's vague theory is that Cook had something wrong with his intestines.

Nonsense, claims Salmond. Cook had suffered a crisis of faith. He was 'disenchanted'. In part, this took the form of whipping his men. Beaglehole writes: 'It was a flogging age, and Cook was a man of his age. ... I have kept no statistics but I have the very strong impression that he did so more severely on this journey than before.' Salmond makes a show of presenting the statistics: forty-four men were given 684 lashes, far more than on Cook's voyages on the *Endeavour* or *Resolution*.

The *Discovery* was an unhappy ship. Denuded of nails it leaked badly, and suffered a plague of rats, especially since Tongans stole the ship's cats. Ill will and resentment were definitely rife at Kealakekua Bay. Cook had tried to take a chief hostage in exchange for the cutter. A crowd gathered. They threw rocks. Cook fired his musket. He retreated to the water's edge. Nowhere to go: the navigator of the world's uncharted oceans couldn't swim.

In the days that followed, a jeering islander appeared on the beach, strutting to and fro in Cook's jacket and trousers. Another wore Cook's hat, and came out on a canoe. He threw stones and smacked his backside. The first part of Cook's body to be returned was a hunk of burned flesh from his thigh. On February 22, as the *Discovery* prepared to leave, a chief presented Cook's feet. And then the tiny expensive ship had somewhere to go, and sailed on.

[February 1, 2009]

Did a Word in the Wrong Ear Kill Cook?

I overlooked a vital piece of information that further supports my thesis that the tragic demise of Captain Cook owed something to low, black farce. All farce is built on the principle of misunderstanding; the wrong word in the wrong ear played its part in Cook's death at Kealakekua Bay in Hawai'i on the morning of February 14, 1779.

Today, Kealakekua 'is reached by a long winding road that plunges down the side of the cliffs, past a sprawling factory where coffee beans are roasted,' writes University of Auckland distinguished professor of Māori Studies and Anthropology, Anne Salmond, in *The Trial of the Cannibal Dog*, her masterful study of Cook. 'Despite its majestic setting, Kealakekua is now quiet, almost a backwater.' But when Cook set anchor there in 1779, it was the seat of old Hawai'ian royalty, heavily populated, with coconut groves lining the beach and a dense forest set in the mountains, 'whence came canoe hulls and the images of the gods', as J.C. Beaglehole writes in his great 1974 biography, *The Life of Captain James Cook*.

Cook and his men arrived to a rapturous welcome. A thousand people canoed or swam out to meet the *Discovery*.

Women flocked to sleep with the sailors; fabulous gifts were presented. Cook took a boat and landed on the beach. Locals lay prostrate on the ground before him. He was regarded as Lono, a god, and made the guest of honour at loud and hilarious feasts. He met the sacred high chief, Kalani'opu'u, who exchanged names with Cook. Salmond's reading is that the ritual also signified they exchanged their 'life force'.

Cook had anchored on January 17. He left on February 4. That pleased the Hawai'ians. Their reception had cooled. But the *Discovery* ran into a gale and the foremast was badly damaged. Cook gave the order to return to Kealakekua for repairs. They anchored again on February 11.

This time no one came out to meet the *Discovery*. Cook landed, and although he was treated with the same veneration and given gifts of food and cloaks, the Hawai'ians were suspicious. Had he returned to make war? Meanwhile, the ship became the object of pilfering. A pair of armourer's tongs ('the fatal attraction of that piece of equipment!' Beaglehole writes) was stolen, recovered, and stolen again. The theft of the ship's cutter was the final straw. Cook cordoned off the bay. He sent Lieutenant Rickman to one end, and himself arrived at Kealakekua with Lieutenant Phillips and nine armed marines. He intended to take Kalani'opu'u hostage in return for the cutter. It was the morning of February 14.

The chief's sons led Cook to his hut. Kalani'opu'u was asleep. Phillips went in to wake him up. Salmond writes: 'A high chief should never be startled awake in this fashion, for his spirit might wander while he was asleep and he could die if he was abruptly woken.' But there were no hard feelings. Kalani'opu'u happily accepted Cook's invitation to board the *Discovery* and walked with him, arm in arm, back to the beach. A crowd gathered. They watched without incident or comment.

And then fate, in the form of farce, intervened. Beaglehole takes up the narrative. 'At the other end of the bay, to keep a canoe from escaping, muskets had been fired – by Rickman among others – and a man killed. The man was Kalimu, a chief of high rank. Another chief, hastening to the ships in indignation to pour out the story to Cook, was disregarded and forthwith made for the beach.'

A moment of 'disregard': was this all it took to turn a peaceful negotiation into a kind of Valentine's Day massacre on February 14? It's a false enterprise to isolate a single incident in the examination of any crime scene, and give it a significance it doesn't deserve. The circumstances leading to Cook's death are complex. His crew were possibly mutinous, and unwilling to help him in a crisis; the islanders in Hawai'i had become suspicious; the theft of the tongs created tensions. 'There was no one cause,' as Salmond writes.

But what might have happened if Cook's crew had bothered to hear out that indignant chief? Would it have altered things, saved Cook's life, led him back to England and a pillowed death in a comfortable bed? Did a simple matter of inattention play a crucial role in bringing Lono to his knees in the surf at Kealakekua?

The disregarded message gained an audience at the beach. Beaglehole: 'It was Cook he wanted, not the crowd. It was the crowd that got the news, spreading like wildfire, not Cook; and the news was enough ... to carry them over the borderline of excitement into attack.' The bloody end came quickly. Cook's life force was extinguished in the shallows.

His genius and incredible achievement as a navigator and explorer remain undiminished. He fixed New Zealand on the map. But perhaps the drama of his death – with its unlikely props and its black comedy of errors – conforms to Gibbon's view of history as 'little more than the register of the crimes, follies and misfortunes of mankind'.

[February 8, 2009]

Down the End of Lonely Street

Robert FitzRoy has returned to Auckland. He slipped back into town a couple of years ago – quietly, unnoticed. I have walked past him most days these past few months without realising it. He finally caught my eye last week. I stopped and stared at the street sign: GOVERNOR FITZROY PLACE.

The city council renamed it in FitzRoy's honour in 2007. He was New Zealand's second governor, replacing William Hobson, who died in office after performing his unfortunate paperwork on the Treaty of Waitangi. FitzRoy arrived in Christmas 1843. His official welcome in Auckland featured a guard of honour, drums, a man shrieking on a fife. But the previous day he slipped away from the ship – quietly, unnoticed – to say his prayers at St Paul's, then in Emily Place, up the hill from Governor Fitzroy Place.

He was England's man in Auckland. In May 1844 he hosted 'a great native feast' in the city, and held talks with Māori ('These visits were tediously prolonged') at Government House. His residence looked over the harbour, and down on a swamp that later became Queen Street. Governor Fitzroy Place follows in his footsteps, the tracks made by the horse he rode in on.

The strangest building on his street is the Mormon Institute of Religion. I went in, sat down, flipped through a student manual of church doctrines: 'Salvation is nothing more nor less than to triumph over all our enemies and put them under our feet.' FitzRoy's enemies always put him under their feet. Even his revival on Auckland's map carries a petty humiliation. Governor Fitzroy Place is a small one-way street, and it leads into the much longer Wakefield Street – named after the family that used its influence to get rid of FitzRoy from New Zealand. He refused to endorse their land swindlings.

He was sacked in 1845. During his brief, disastrous tenure, the new colony had gone to something regarded as worse than the dogs – it threatened to go to the Māori. Te Rauparaha took scalps at the Wairau massacre, Hone Heke burnt down Kororareka. FitzRoy, too, was set alight, in effigy, in Wellington and Nelson, by settlers who were outraged at his leniency towards Te Rauparaha.

'Poor FitzRoy,' wrote Charles Darwin. FitzRoy had been his captain on the *Beagle*. 'His poor mind,' wrote FitzRoy's widow, Maria. He cut his throat with a razor at their home in London. It was a Sunday morning. Maria asked if he had slept well. 'He complained of the light and I said we must contrive something to keep it out. ... He got up before I did and went to his dressing room, kissing Laura as he passed, and did not lock the door at first.'

In 1954 Darwin's granddaughter called upon Laura Fitz-Roy. 'I remember well,' she wrote, 'the look of her crowded Victorian drawing room, dominated by a large white marble bust of her father – a remarkable face, sensitive, severe, fanatical, combining a strength of purpose with some weakness or uncertainty.' The face of a manic depressive. Since two FitzRoy biographies – one ridiculously sympathetic, the other ridiculously hostile – appeared in 2003 I've very nearly come to love FitzRoy. In England I visited his grave, and stepped inside the house where he killed himself. He was so hapless. He was the man who could never triumph. His theme was disappointment.

As a devout Christian who believed in the *Genesis* fable of creation, he felt betrayed when Darwin – his passenger and close friend for five years – published *The Origin of Species*. On an earlier voyage, he had got it into his head to bring four natives from Tierra del Fuego to England. That had ended in tragedy. In his final appointment, he headed the new meteorological office; his forecasts were mocked, stupidly and fiercely, in *The Times*.

His two years in New Zealand were just another unhappiness. The tallest building on Governor Fitzroy Place is the AUT Business School. Its best minds are right now analysing the recession; FitzRoy inherited a colony strapped for cash, and his financial solution included raising land and customs tax. You could describe it as unpopular.

Most of the rest of the street houses AUT's art department.

There's a life drawing class, a TV studio, and a St Paul Street Gallery. It had an exhibition about Māori dance when I visited – photographs, archive film, a nineteenth-century lithographic panorama. I talked to gallery assistant Melissa Laing in her narrow office and asked whether she had any knowledge about Governor FitzRoy. 'To tell you the truth,' she said, 'I've none.' Her PhD examined the relationship between visual art and international air travel. 'I'm a 1980s-onwards kind of person,' she said.

I showed her the panorama in the gallery. It was a depiction of FitzRoy's 'great native feast' in Auckland. The caption referred to 'an immense quantity of dried shark intended as food'. You could see Mount Eden and Mount Hobson, flax, ferns, a swamp, huts, wagons, the chief police magistrate, thousands of Māori, a bare tattooed bum – and there, stiff and stunted astride a black horse, poor Robert FitzRoy. He wore a high-collared jacket. You couldn't see his throat.

[June 21, 2009]

Did a New Zealand Summer
Kill Cook?

It rained. December was a drag; there were furious gales, the *Endeavour* was driven out of sight of land at the top of North Cape, and struck a rock in the middle of the night – Cook ran on to the deck in his drawers. 'Heavy showers,' he wrote in his journal. 'Blowing weather ... storms ... hurricanes.' The first tourists to spend a summer in New Zealand experienced the truth of that popular joke: the winterless north.

The summer of 1769 to 1770 was any summer. Rata and pohutakawa mad with crimson, plump godwits lined up on the mudflats, mangroves sucking at the tide, the lazy curl of smoke rising from beaches, rain. But there were also white men, 'strange sea-goblins' to their hosts, pointing sticks that boomed and flared, arriving on a ship which flapped like a bird. Landfall in New Zealand was in spring, on the East Coast; summer, in the first week of December, began with sunshine in the Bay of Islands. A chief presented Cook with gifts of large mackerel. The crew caught mullet, shark and stingray. They were also in the mood for a drink and a potato: three men were punished with a dozen lashes for digging up gardens and filching kumara, and the whip came down again on culprits who stole twelve gallons of rum.

White sand, warm earth. But the *Endeavour* headed north on December 5, towards a storm at sea. It calmed on Christmas Day. The cook served an excellent 'goose pye'. Joseph Banks shot gannets for the dish, which food historian David Veart speculates was made from a recipe by eighteenth-century cookbook writer Hannah Glasse. 'Take half a quarter of an ounce of mace beat fine, a large teaspoonful of beaten pepper, three teaspoonfuls of salt, and season your fowl. ... Put half a pound of butter on the top, and lay on the lid.' Serve with colossal amounts of rum. Banks' journal, Boxing Day: 'All heads ached with yesterday's debauch.' It rained.

The ship rounded the Cape, then sped south along the North Island's west coast in the first week of the new year. Through another storm, they saw the hunched mangroves at the entrance of Kaipara Harbour, and hundreds of gannets plunging into the water off the coast of Kawhia. Look at that, said Cook, and wrote down: 'Mt Egmont.' Creamy snow, black sand.

Onwards, to the South Island. Cook finally set anchor – sails were split, the Endeavour creaked and the crew stank – at two in the afternoon on January 15 at Ship Cove in Marlborough Sounds. It became a favourite holiday home during his next two voyages. He would be killed on today's date, in a kind of Valentine Day's massacre, in 1779 in Hawai'i; by then he was sick and tired, at least half-mad. But in that first golden February in the Sounds, he was fit, forty-one, happy. He loved the calm bay, the amazing sound of birdland. It was here that Banks wrote his famous line about the dawn chorus: 'The most melodious wild musick I have ever heard.' They set up camp for three weeks and enjoyed perfect weather.

Cook put his men to work – caulking the hull with tar and oil, cutting grass for the sheep, drying the sails, filling casks with fresh water, rebaking the ship's bread to kill an infestation of weevils – but there was also time to relax. They feasted on delicious shellfish. They swam. They shot shags. No one got flogged. The tide raking the sand, soft evenings beneath the Southern Cross... Idyllic, lovely, except for the sensation caused by evidence of cannibalism. Their hosts held up the bone of a human arm, licked their lips, and demonstrated eating the 'dainty bit'. Māori are lower than animals, said Banks, and promptly traded an old pair of his white linen drawers for the preserved head of a fourteen-year-old boy.

They sailed again on February 5, into another storm, the sky dark and gloomy. Water and land submitted to English words – Cook Strait, Banks Peninsula. On February 17, near Akaroa, they saw a couple of people sitting on top of a grassy hill; according to the author Anne Salmond they didn't see another human soul for the remainder of their time in New Zealand. What did the two Māori make of a wooden bird flapping across the Pacific on that summer's day? Was the grass warm and ticklish? The vision disappeared, headed

further south. Banks was convinced they were about to dis-
cover a new continent. They discovered Stewart Island.

The tourists turned north, did Fiordland and the West
Coast. You can guess what that was like: they experienced
the truth of another droll joke, summertime in New Zealand.
It rained. March was a drag. Banks fell as sick as a dog, then
ate a dog – the hindquarters roasted, the forequarters baked
in a pie, the viscera tortured into a haggis. He preferred the
delicacy of albatross. His recipe: 'Skin the bird, and soak in
salt water overnight. ... Stew until tender.'

The nights began to cool. Autumn was approaching. Cook
announced it was time to return to England. They had been
at sea since August 1768. They left on the last day of March,
from Cape Farewell. 'Next morning,' writes Cook's greatest
biographer, J.C. Beaglehole, 'New Zealand was lost in rain
and cloud.'

[February 14, 2010]

CRIME

Dixon in Summer

S ummer, always summer, in the dismal story of Antonie Ronnie Dixon. A hot parched day was collapsing into the cool of evening on January 21, 2003, when he mutilated two women with a samurai sword at his home in Thames – a packet of Round Wine biscuits on the kitchen table, blood in the cat bowl next to a box of Whiskas cat food. He drove to Auckland, parked behind a Caltex service station just after midnight, gave the fingers to a passer-by, and shot the man dead. He stood trial in 2005. It began the day after Waitangi Day and lasted seven weeks; bright sunlight squinted through the venetian blinds of an upstairs courtroom. He was found guilty and sentenced to life imprisonment. His lawyers won an appeal. There was a retrial. A jury once again found him guilty. Earlier this month, just as temperatures began soaring to forty degrees, he was found dead in his prison cell.

He will remain one of the great demons of modern New Zealand life, forever loathed, fixed in the public memory as the mong who took too much P and went berserk. His sword, with its long thin blade snapped in two at the tip because of the force of impact when it struck bone, was placed inside a glass case as an exhibit at his trial. It forever hovers in the air next to his despised name; his black, scratched, short-barrelled fully automatic lightweight submachine gun failed to hold the imagination, even though it was the murder weapon.

His own death was an apparent suicide. It was a long time in coming, a promise finally kept. On the night of his crimes he invited police to kill him. At sentencing, he clapped his hands and hooted, 'Bring back the electric chair!' He had already made one clumsy attempt to top himself when psychiatrist Dr Karl Jansen told the court, 'He may yet end his life. I think the risk is high.'

Dixon admitted the sword attacks, the fatal shooting, the firing at police and the taking of a hostage, but pleaded not guilty on grounds of insanity. Jansen agreed. Was he right about that, too?

Everyone who stands trial acts as a kind of host. In 2005, Dixon drew big crowds wanting to hear the exact details of his methamphetamine rage. They also came to see if he would display visible signs of lunacy. He obliged by rolling his eyes around in his head. Also, he modelled an incredible haircut. I studied it from the public gallery and wrote: 'It looked as though he had borrowed it from a small boy. Brown and flat, it rested on the very top of his shaved head like a light nest. So light that it almost seemed to tremble above his head – it was a haircut that wanted out, but was doomed to follow him around.'

In short, he looked like a clown. He became a laughing

stock. The eyes settled after the first couple of days, and his hair grew back. For the remainder of the trial, he stank out the courtroom with blasts from his flatulent bum, carved his name in wood, and kept his head down. Was he listening to the evidence? One of the women he sliced with his sword was called as a witness. She spoke about falling in love with him, and described a charming, kind and exciting man.

She also spoke about the days leading up to the attack. A summer countdown, the sky stuffed with sunshine, the dry, yellow fields of Thames. She went to the Big Day Out concert on Friday. She visited Dixon's ex-wife on Saturday. 'I don't remember Sunday and Monday. And then Tuesday ... Tuesday was Tuesday.' She put it another way: 'There was just so much screaming and blood and silver.'

He was sentenced on a morning in autumn. That afternoon I met with Dr Ian Goodwin, a psychiatrist who had interviewed Dixon more than anyone else. He was sure Dixon had been coached to display symptoms of mental illness. He said, 'Tony's not mad in the psychiatric sense. He's a person with a damaged personality, with a paranoid view of the world, and has great difficulty maintaining normal relationships, and had a raging P habit for a while.' He talked about a man who was 'good at reading people. He's socially prescient. He anticipates things very well.'

But he also said, 'When he was about seventeen he was seen by a psychiatrist, and his phrase was: "Dixon seems devoid of moral or social conscience." I think that's probably right.' And: 'When I first met him, he asked me to kill him.'

You can dismiss him as bad rubbish, and duly wish him good riddance. You can call him vermin, or a scumbag, or any of the other usual, easily reached terms of contempt. 'In this game,' Dr Goodwin had said, 'people get easily demonised. They get turned into evil monsters. They're really just people. They have various aspects to their personality.' You can list a few of the 'aspects': charming, prescient, damaged, violent, remorseless. And you can see him allowed to disappear into an oblivion of his own making – a dead man staggering towards one last, intolerable summer. Antonie Ronnie Dixon was forty.

[February 22, 2009]

Whore Adite

O n a lovely autumn morning earlier this month, a small
black handbag was placed on the witness stand in
courtroom six at the High Court in Auckland.

— Is that your handbag?

— Yes.

— Did you take it with you that morning?

— Yes.

— What did you put in it?

— Condoms, lubricants, baby oil and lip gloss. I was on
my way to work the daytime shift.

And then defence lawyer Louise Freyer asked the court
clerk to produce another exhibit. The clerk slipped on a pair
of white gloves and you could hear the sharp little sound
of a knife scuffing the surface of a table. It was placed next
to the handbag. The woman in the witness stand began to
cry. When she was told to pick up the murder weapon, her
hands trembled.

She wore her dark hair in a fringe and said that the name
she adopted as a prostitute was Shania. Her real name was
Dionne, a girl from Glenfield who got married and bought
a house in Helensville, but lost custody of her children and

rented in Beach Haven – her trial was a directory of Auckland addresses. You heard about drives over the harbour bridge, a game of golf, walks on the beach. Auckland in the summer of 2007; Waitangi Day was on a Tuesday.

Dionne stabbed her ex-boyfriend Reece to death that holiday morning after he made her a cup of tea at his Parnell flat. Newspaper headline two days later: POLICE CLOSE IN ON KILLER. She was arrested the following day.

Reece was thirty-eight, had worked in advertising. Dionne was thirty-seven, had worked as a hairdresser and a belly dance instructor. They met in 2004 at Mustangs Gentlemans Club. Crown prosecutor Kevin Glubb said to her in cross-examination, 'He was part of the woodwork there. He had access to the staff kitchen.' And then Glubb, fit, redhaired, purposeful, an ex-cop, tried his hand at sarcasm.

– If there were a frequent flyer programme for parlours, he'd qualify for a gold card, wouldn't he?

– They actually do have loyalty cards.

Her answer surprised Glubb, flattened his joke, but the jury smiled anyway. They needed a laugh. Their dozen faces advertised an Auckland census – they were from India, China, the Pacific Islands. Only three were European.

They were told about blood splatter. They were told about Dionne's 'borderline personality'. They were also told about her dreams. 'I'm sorry,' Justice Graham Lang told Freyer, 'but where's this going?' She'd wanted to ask Dionne about her 'premonitions'. He'd interrupted: 'Is this relevant?'

Freyer, who always wears a matching pearl necklace and earrings to court, somehow talked him into it. Yes, said Dionne, she once dreamed every night for an entire year about planes landing and taking off. After her arrest, she was taken to the women's prison near Auckland Airport. Planes landing, planes taking off... 'I'm a very spiritual person,' she said.

But there was another, deeper secret life moving throughout the trial: sex. Reece and Dionne formed a relationship, moved into together. She said he called her 'his perfect woman', complimented her 'porn vixen's body'. She texted him about clients at Mustangs – a man in a wheelchair ('a spastic'), a man in high heels and lipstick ('stop laughing').

Reece continued booking other prostitutes. He told Dionne about a Scottish girl ('tight little bum'), an Australian girl ('nice tits'). They broke up. He moved to Parnell. She visited, spent an afternoon drinking wine and smoking dope. There was talk of a threesome – as Shania, Dionne had put on lesbian shows. 'You'd cover your face with your hair. It was just acting.' Dionne texted a Mustangs colleague to visit her and Reece. The fee was four hundred dollars. But the girl decided she wanted to stay home and watch TV: Saturday night in Auckland.

Dionne said he had 'rough' sex with her that night, taunted her about the Scottish girl. She left the flat, and keyed his car. She wrote three words, two sentences. CHEATA. And, WHORE ADITE.

— What were you trying to spell?

— Addict. I'm dyslexic.

She killed him the next time she saw him. Glubb said she planned it, took the knife from her home. Freyer had Dionne demonstrate that it didn't fit inside her handbag: the ugly grey stainless-steel handle stuck out the top. Dionne said they'd argued. He took a shower. She saw a knife in his kitchen. 'I just wanted to hurt him.' She stabbed him in the arm. 'He slipped and fell on me and the knife went into his chest.'

The jury found her guilty of murder. There will be an appeal. Sentencing is set for this Friday. Another day in court, the official process, the quiet, devastated families. So many private details had been tracked down and tipped out. Reece's last ATM withdrawals were $1,016 for shoes and a shirt at Satori, and, at 2.57 a.m. on Waitangi Day 2007, $195 for a girl at Famous Flora's. Sex and dreams and Auckland, and a story about broken love.

[May 31, 2009]

Weatherston in Winter

Winter was Weatherston, his trial in June and July providing a weird background noise to the cold days and dark nights, a noise that rose in volume and never seemed to end – the noise of Weatherston's own voice. He had murdered his ex-girlfriend Sophie Elliott in a rage so vicious and prolonged that it went beyond causing death. He tried to rid the Earth of her flesh. He talked as though he had broken a vase, and needed to remind the courtroom it was only a vase. Now, in springtime, he returns for his last appearance in public. Justice Judith Potter will sentence Clayton Weatherston on Tuesday.

The trial began on June 24, delayed for two days because defence lawyer Greg King entered a late submission to stop the jury from seeing photos of Elliott's mutilated body. No, said the judge. King went to the Court of Appeal. No, it said, describing the submission as 'hopeless'. Weatherston pleaded not guilty, giving his defence as provocation. The trial ended on July 22, when the jury delivered the only possible verdict.

Four weeks, but the trial had relayed an average horror until Weatherston took the stand for five days. Wednesday,

Thursday; then Monday, Tuesday, Wednesday. You thought: please, someone, anyone, make him stop. But he wouldn't stop. It was like a monologue, detailed and epic – 'exhaustive', as he put it. The five amazing days felt longer than the trial, as long as winter. Rain turned lawns to mud. Trees froze as hard as bone. Throughout, there was Weatherston, a blithe spirit at the High Court of Christchurch, articulate and patient, helpful and sensitive, casual and amused, concerned with logic and accuracy, his occupation blandly described as 'former economics tutor', thirty-three years old with a PhD, but like a genuinely clever child wanting to convince, talking quite freely about his version of the events that led him to murder.

He was something new – nothing as fancy as an enigma, nothing as simple as a 'pink-eyed, posturing pervert', to quote the purple, puerile prose of a newspaper columnist. A psychiatrist said Weatherston committed the murder in a state of disassociated rage. He remained disassociated in court. He knew his actions were wrong, but under the circumstances they were perfectly natural. Elliott had pushed him over the edge. Once that was accepted, then people would see his response was unfortunate, but within reason. They'd say: Yes, that makes sense. They'd say: Fair play.

It wasn't gall, it wasn't arrogance; it was worse than that. It wasn't a performance, it wasn't anything resembling entertainment. It was his search for understanding. Five days after the murder, and awaiting his first court appearance, he wrote in a letter to a friend, 'I am nervous about court on Thursday and annoyed my side will not be made public.' In another letter, sent to his mother from prison, he wrote: 'When everyone hears my side of the story I'll be understood. Don't worry, mum.'

'Annoyed', 'Don't worry, Mum' – an indignant child, a stoic son. On TV3, *60 Minutes* reporter Alison Horwood displayed a six-page curriculum vitae that she had received from Weatherston. She flipped the pages; you saw round, schoolboy handwriting, and a sincere remark about his family: 'Two awesome parents.' His mother told Horwood, 'All he has ever wanted to be is a good boy.'

Clayt and Soph were a couple for five, six months. He said she was abusive, bad news; he was stressed, couldn't breathe. He lost the prize he most valued: control. He tried to regain it in court. 'I just want to explain the situation,' he said. 'That's what is in my control.' But he had already taken full and exhilarating control in the act of murder. In an earlier argument, he had called her fat, ugly, a whore. He told a friend: 'I gave her my hate.' He had much more to give. On the morning of his thirty-second birthday, he browsed Elliott's Facebook photo album at his university office. And then he went to her house with a knife in his laptop case. She was leaving town to start a new job. He wanted the last word. He got it. He wanted her out of his life. He succeeded. He was a man head over heels in hate.

A witness told the court, 'He said he couldn't believe how

horrible she was and how he had let someone so negative into his life.' Weatherston, in that letter sent five days after the killing: 'I am sorry that such a horrible person has been glorified in the media.' The next sentences: 'That is our society. It will blow over.' And then: 'Not going to dwell on uncontrollables but rather on staying positive.'

The life and death of Sophie Elliott, twenty-two, waved aside. Weatherston, at trial, talking about her murder: 'It was the ultimate self-destructive thing.' His self-destruction, his grief, his tragedy – Weatherston, always Weatherston, who needed, said a psychiatrist, to have a positive thought whenever he turned off a light. 'The ritual was the same if he took the lid off a jar or a hung a towel on the rail.' He turned off a life – just another inanimate object – on January 9, 2008. A summer murder, a winter monologue, remorseless and hopeless; in spring, on Tuesday, a disappearance.

[September 13, 2009]

A Call for Better Standards
of Email Fraud

All that stands between Nigeria's infamous email fraud criminals and the raking in of even more money is a good subeditor. Are they taking on staff? Are the offices fully air-conditioned? Do they contribute towards KiwiSaver? I travelled to Nigeria on assignment in 2003, when its capital city, Abuja, hosted the Commonwealth Heads of Government Meeting, and have fond memories of the people, the food, and the smoke from fires on the side of the road to scare away snakes. But the command of English was eccentric. I ordered bush meat – barbecued and heavily peppered goat – at Peculiar Restaurant. I watched children file into Pinky And The Brain Primary School. Perhaps some of the graduates found work in the email fraud trade.

I was very nearly taken for a ride earlier this month by a Nigerian scam. An email arrived from a friend. It was shocking. She said she'd been held up at gunpoint in London, and was in desperate need of funds to return to New Zealand – eight hundred pounds, she estimated, would cover hotel bills, a cab to the airport, and sundry expenses. I thought: poor girl! I decided to send five hundred dollars and then felt guilty of miserliness. But her email was addressed to 'undisclosed recipients'; other people were bound to chip in and help cover her costs. I replied immediately and asked for her bank account details. Then I reread her email.

She wrote: 'Hi dear, I'm sorry for this odd request because it might get to you too urgent but it's due to the situation of things right now. I'm stranded in London, united kingdom, i came down here for a short vacation got mugged at GUN POINT last night, worse of it is that bags, cash and cards and my cell phone were stolen, it's such a crazy experience for me, i need help flying back home, the authorities are not being 100% supportive but the good thing is i still have my passport and return ticket ... Please i need you to loan me some money, will would definitely refund you as soon as i get back home, i promise but don't know how much you would be able to spare.'

As fiction it was direct and compelling. A young New Zealand woman mugged in London, vulnerable, penniless, traumatised. I imagined the villain as a pitiless and pock-marked yob, and staff at the New Zealand High Commission shaking their heads and saying, 'There's nothing we can do.' But I began to worry about something else: her mangled, reckless English. The alarmed capital letters and the descent into lower case were minor lapses. How, though, to explain 'might get to you too urgent', and 'will would definitely re-fund you'? We all make excuses for our friends; I reasoned that the careless writing was due to trauma. 'It's such a crazy experience.' You try thinking straight, never mind writing crisp, correct sentences, when you've been mugged at GUN POINT.

But there's a difference between trauma and plain stupidity. Rereading the email, I finally thought: hang on. I knew my friend as intelligent, educated, a smart whip. Could a 'crazy experience' so quickly reduce her to write like a dunce? I emailed again, asking if it was really her. No reply. I tracked her down by phone the next day. She was at her home in Devonport. Hackers had gained access to her Gmail account. Friends, family and other 'undisclosed recipients' were all terribly concerned.

The scam goes back at least twelve months. Facebook users as well as email accounts are routinely hacked. It's always the same narrative – a damsel in distress, usually in London. An earlier variation was played out in February 2009, when Britain's justice minister, Jack Straw, was targeted by fraudsters, who used his email address to send an SOS to about two hundred of his constituents. It claimed Straw was stranded in Nigeria. 'I misplaced my wallet on my way to the hotel where my money and other valuable things were kept. ... I would like you to assist me with a soft loan urgently to settle my hotel bills and get myself back home.' Rather sadly, no one offered him assistance.

There's a sucker born every minute – I've read about a gullible fool in Arizona who was twice parted from his money by 'friends' mugged in London – but competent English could double that birth rate to every thirty seconds. Nigeria's email fraudsters lose business because of their incompetence. Vladimir Nabokov wrote in *Lolita*, 'You can always count on a murderer for a fancy prose style.' You can always count on a Nigerian email criminal for a ridiculous prose style. They really ought to employ staff with basic editing skills. I can recommend any of the journalism students at Wintec. As editor in residence I vouch for their abilities, but worry about their future prospects. Newsrooms are shrinking. Where will they find work? How far are they prepared to travel? Could they stomach bush meat at Peculiar Restaurant?

I would have waited for details on where to send my five hundred dollars if only the viral scam had bothered to compose better sentences. 'Thanks anyway,' said my friend in Devonport. It was nice talking to her. She said she was leaving New Zealand at the end of the month to live in London.

[May 9, 2010]

An Incident in Motueka

A great New Zealand sentence appeared earlier this month in *The Nelson Mail*. It had everything, and nothing. It had petty crime. It had sport in the background. It was set in a provincial town. And it had sound: the laconic nasal honk of New Zealand truth. It read: 'Three Nelson men decided to burgle the Motueka Golf Club because they were bored.'

In just fourteen words – no time for the leisure of commas or the nuance of hyphens – this opening sentence of an inside-page court story managed to pack in and leave hanging as much drama, farce and pathos as a novel. Good journalism constantly reads like fiction, or at least a first draft. Something important, something working itself under the surface, was at play in the revelation that three Nelson men decided to burgle the Motueka Golf Club because they were bored.

It dared to confirm the sheer boringness of New Zealand life. Everyone knows what that feels like, and looks like. The lights out in the curtained houses, the same old faces on the main street in broad, bright daylight. The umbrellas on the sideline of rugby fields on cold Saturday mornings, the town halls booked out on Saturday nights for Scottish highland dancing. At three a.m., a possum hissing in a tree; at dawn, the moan of a fat cow. All that lovely, empty, dull and maddening paradise... Teenagers, who have an acute sense of boredom, suffer the worst of it.

No age was given for the three Nelson men who decided to burgle the Motueka Golf Club because they were bored. Only one was named: Shaun Robert Taylor. He pleaded guilty to a charge of burglary. Police prosecutor Sergeant Chris Stringer gave evidence.

'Mr Stringer said that at 6.30 a.m. on April 19, a member of the public alerted the police to the burglary after hearing the burglar alarm go off and seeing three men run across the car park. One of the men was carrying the club's cash register, which he dropped. Another man was seen carrying a crowbar.'

A dawn raid, in sunny Motueka, population 7845. April 19 was a Monday; what had the three men got up to that weekend? Were they bored to the back teeth? Did boredom keep the three men awake all that Sunday night, until it drove them so crazed that they jumped in the car, tooled around town, and began to regard the Motueka Golf Club with wild surmise?

A golf course is a grassy vacant lot. There are over 400 golf courses in New Zealand, over 400 grassy vacant lots. As they stood at the edge of the yawning greens in darkness, three Nelson men decided to burgle the Motueka Golf

Club because they were bored, but it could have been worse. In February, Benjamin James Kelly, 18, and an unnamed 'associate' were charged with damaging the greens at the Invercargill Golf Club. The 'associate' defecated in one of the holes before replacing the flag.

Kelly told police he was 'caught up in the moment'. Maybe the exhilaration of a friend dumping a load in a golf hole was one way of staving off the boringness of Invercargill; in Nelson, Taylor and his two 'associates' experienced the thrill of the chase. According to the *Mail*: 'Mr Stringer said the men were seen driving away. The police located the car on an empty section and saw three men jump over fences into sections. The three were later caught near the Motueka saltwater baths.'

The saltwater baths of Motueka are famous and amazing. They are refreshed with the tide. They were built in 1938 (bathers were afraid of sharks), closed down in 2002, but reopened in 2005 and registered as a historic site. They were the scene of the arrest of three men who decided to burgle the Motueka Golf Club because they were bored. The story continues: 'Mr Stringer said a window at the club had been smashed to gain entry.' And then the fatal admission: 'Taylor told the police it was a spontaneous decision to burgle the golf club, because they were bored.'

Bored, in Motueka? How is that even possible, considering the existence and appeal of the Motueka Pottery Workshop, the Motueka Parents and Babies Group, and the various ongoing fun activities coordinated by the Nelson Tasman Youth Workers Collective? Boredom is a kind of sin. We drone: 'If you're bored, it's your own fault.' No further discussion is allowed. 'Life, friends, is boring,' wrote the poet John Berryman. 'We must not say so.'

New Zealand is full of boring drunks. Kelly said he was drunk when his anonymous 'associate' made an odious deposit at the Invercargill Golf Club. New Zealand's teenage drinking culture has attracted a lot of earnest comment this year. We can legislate against alcohol, and drug use. But how do we legislate against boredom? Is the Law Commission working on recommendations?

The story in *The Nelson Mail* ends: 'Judge Tony Zohrab remanded Taylor for sentencing on July 13 and told him all sentencing options were open, including prison.' Good luck to him. Wider circumstances – his background, his character, his standing in the community – will form the pre-sentencing report. The judge will also take into account that he told the truth.

[June 27, 2010]

LANGUAGE

Scott Optican. Scott Optican. Scott Optican.

Scott Optican is coming to a crime story near you. Whenever his name appears in print or on radio or TV, it's always either followed or preceded by his title and place of occupation, and so he is variously announced as an 'Auckland University assistant law professor', 'Auckland Faculty of Law assistant professor', 'Auckland University senior law lecturer', 'Auckland University criminal law expert' or – a personal favourite – 'Auckland University criminologist'.

Scott Optican. It's a good name. It has a confidence and a sense of achievement about it. It's the kind of name that might belong to a human relations manager, or the author of solid but unspectacular thrillers sold in airports. You'd feel reassured if your GP were called Scott Optican.

Scott Optican, Scott Optican. If you've seen his name once, you'll have seen it twice. He is forever in the newspapers. He is as regular as the crossword and the weather forecast. You could say he owns criminal law in New Zealand. Complex issues, even only vaguely complex issues, require his presence. He has a valuable commodity to sell: an expert opinion. He has been brought in to give his expert opinion on Tony Veitch, the Privy Council, the four English rugby players accused of raping a woman in an Auckland hotel, David Bain, the Serious Fraud Office, the theft of war medals from the National Army Museum, Peter Ellis, the so-called 'terror raids' in the Urewera, the Police Complaints Authority, Brent Todd, habeas corpus and Scott Watson.

Scott Optican, Scott Optican, Scott Optican. Journalists in countless newsrooms chant his name. Someone will advise, 'You should call Scott Optican for an expert opinion.' Someone will ask, 'Does anyone have a number for Scott Optican?' A notebook flips open, a pen is poised above the paper; a phone rings in an office in Auckland University, and a pleasant voice answers: 'Scott Optican.'

Scott Optican, Scott Optican, Scott Optican, Scott Optican. His name is a guarantee of expert opinion. He explains fine points; he educates, informs, performs a public service, pro bono. He is like an agony aunt. He may say something bland, like this comment about sub judice material appearing on the internet: 'The flow and dissemination of information is very difficult to control.' He may say something critical, like this remark about the Police Complaints Authority: 'Its procedures and mechanisms essentially defeat or undermine confidence in its purpose for being.' Typically, he walks on midway through a story and takes the stage for two or three paragraphs. Sometimes he makes only a cameo appearance and is quoted indirectly, but at least it serves the real purpose of the story: it features the magic words 'Scott Optican.'

Scott Optican, Scott Optican, Scott Optican, Scott

Optican, Scott Optican. Said only reasonably fast, his name sounds like a single polysyllabic word that might describe a literary technique. 'Exam question two: Compare and contrast the scotoptican rhythms in the later verse of Eliot with the earlier verse of Yeats.' Said a great many times over the year in print and on radio and TV, his name casts a reliable spell. But what do we know about him? The public are only presented with his name, his various ranks, his expert opinion. How did he become Scott Optican?

Scott Optican, Scott Optican, Scott Optican, Scott Optican, Scott Optican, Scott Optican. His name, plainly, is American. What other country would produce someone called Scott Optican? He spent the formative years of establishing his expert opinion as a student at Berkeley and Harvard, and also at Cambridge. He arrived in Auckland in 1992. A customs official, scanning his passport, would have been the first New Zealander – but by no means the last – to read the name: 'Scott Optican'.

Scott Optican, etc. Does he ever worry that overexposure might damage his good name? As the media's resident academic on issues of criminal law, he risks being regarded as part of the furniture – a comfortable footstool, a dusty ornament. The public may eventually shrug and say, 'There he goes again with his expert opinion. Boring old Scott Optican.'

Why does he put himself through it? Isn't he aware of the jealousy and rage that he inspires among other academics in the same field? Doesn't he mind having his quotes mangled, taken out of context, used to fit the substandard narratives of all journalism? Doesn't he know that the whole process cheapens his name? The media are quite capable of deserting him in a flash. One of his Auckland University colleagues, Paul Buchanan, was forever being quoted for his expert opinion on international relations, but after Buchanan was sacked for sending an inappropriate email to a student his phone never rang again.

And yet the demand on an expert's time is so flattering. For an academic, maintaining a media presence is a kind of calling card. It's good for business, and it's easier and faster than publishing papers in esoteric journals. It's an enticement, an entrapment.

Scott Optican – assistant law professor, senior law lecturer, criminal law expert, criminologist – is coming to a crime story near you, unless he does the unthinkable, unless he rebels, draws a line in the sand, withholds his expert opinion, and shocks his many callers by uttering the two words that never seem to have passed his lips: 'No comment.'

[November 23, 2008]

Spell Chek

This is how it ends: not with a bang but a whimper. Wrong, bad and downright lousy spelling is one of the few growth industries in this age of economic collapse. It's a clear sign of ruin and decay. All year a very clear sign – in white capital letters, chalked on a blackboard – has stood outside a popular Auckland fish and chip shop. It reads: CRAYFISH WHILE YOU WHAITE.

Spelling so downright lousy is almost ingenious. I've marvelled at it, tried to understand how it came about, as I've scoffed crayfish and whaited. I haven't minded whaiteing. I'd even describe it as a rewarding whaite. The blackboard sign presents an intellectual challenge, and it's also quite nice to look at. There's a visible pride in the handwriting – the letters are chalked with style and flourish, especially the lovely looping 'l'. The author's hand is just as confident with every stroke of that last weird word.

But how to explain the misspelling? All crime scene investigations disassemble the evidence; close analysis identifies the deadly agent behind the blackboard atrocity as the word 'while'. Something about it captivated the author, intoxicated him, drugged his senses, led him wildly astray. He couldn't leave it alone. He felt a powerful need to molest it, take the 'H' and the 'E' with him when he chalked in the final word of his sentence.

A rogue 'H' appears in another of my favourite signs of 2009. What is it about that letter? It's firm, upright, a solid piece of architecture, and it ought to know its place. But there it is, barging like a hooligan into a sign written in enormous black capital letters on the back of a building overlooking the Auckland eastern suburbs railway line. It advertises a business which supplies water for swimming pools. It reads: CHRYSTAL CLEAR WATERS.

I suppose it's possible that this business, as well as the fish and chip shop that offers you crayfish while you whaite, is owned by a migrant who has English only as a second language. But I assume Air New Zealand, as our national airline, is operated and serviced by people who have received a childhood education in English. On a recent domestic flight I was kept entertained by a general knowledge quiz, which played on screens throughout the aircraft. One question asked, 'Name the famous novelist whose father fed her a midday meal of potatoes without meat.' Interesting. Who? Passengers were asked to choose from a multiple choice: 'Jackie Collins, Iris Murdoch or Charlotte Bront.'

That would be the Charlotte Bront who wrote *Jane Eyr*, and whose sister Emily Bront wrote *Wuthering Hights*. A few seconds later on flight NZ426, the quiz answer flashed up, obstinate in its declaration that one of the most famous, loved and taught writers in literary history was indeed someone called 'Charlotte Bront'. Oh well. At least it wasn't Charlotte Bronth.

The airline's quiz compiler was on the right track – dear old Mrs Gaskell, the Victorian biographer, wrote of Charlotte and Emily's father, 'He had grown to gigantic proportions on potatoes; he knew no reason why his daughters should fare differently' – but the misspelling of Charlotte Brontë is the mistake of a complete dummy.

Individual blame only goes so far. The Bront gaff, as well as WHAITE and CHRYSTAL, suggests a wider disturbance in the body politic. Wrong, bad and downright lousy spelling is bound to occur right now: literacy is one of the first casualties of a recession.

Job losses, pay freezes, pay cuts and all the rest of it have created a widespread kind of mental rigor mortis. Across the land, staff morale is at an all-time low: the abandoned desks, the increased workload, the glass ceiling at ankle height. It can take a monumental effort to achieve the simplest tasks. The pressure and anxiety become intolerable. Standards begin to drop. Who can be bothered to monitor the finer details of work performance? Is there anyone still employed to monitor the finer details of work performance?

Western civilisation depends on the constant maintenance of two dense, complex systems of communication: numerals and language. Numerals have failed us, got us into this mess – finance is bunk. Language was the next to fall. New

Zealand has an impeccable role model in the shape of John Key. When I interviewed him a year before he came to power, he told me he had a near photographic memory for … numbers. But words have always failed him. 'I can't tell you how good this feels!' he said on election night. I doubt he can tell us how anything feels. His incessant mangling of the English language – 'I passionely believe', etc – makes him a man for our times.

Another sign is explicit about the connection between recession and illiteracy. It appeared in the window of one of my local shops a few weeks ago. The sign has gone now, and so has the shop – it sold a strange combination of mobile phones and women's jewellery. It opened in 2007. Business often appeared to be brisk. But it slowed down last year, and I hardly saw a soul cross its doorway this year. The end was nigh. The owner daubed a sign in black capital letters. It read: CLOSEING DOWN SALE.

[June 7, 2009]

Wea've It All

Yes, another study of misspelling in pubic. In an earlier column I marvelled at recent crazed instances of the English language gone wrong in full view of innocent passers-by – a blackboard menu that read CRAYFISH WHILE YOU WHAITE, a shop sign that sadly advised its CLOSEING DOWN SALE. Readers could hardly whaite to respond. Thanks to everyone who emailed, and cheers to Wellington author Mary Mountier, who posted a copy of her new book. Its sub-title: 'An easy guide to correct punctuation.' Its title: *Your Joking*.

In her introduction she writes: 'Roadside signs, advertisements and menus are still a rich source for mistakes.' Yes. John sent in a photo of an incredible roof in Whangarei. In giant capital letters, a sign is painted on the roof. It boasts: WEA'VE IT ALL! 'Took it in 2006 and it's still there,' wrote John. 'Not just a sign on a board but a whole roof that boasts supremacy in equipment hire. ... This will be a proud sight to view from the new rugby stadium being constructed for the World Cup.'

Barry of Christchurch offered three examples. 'Imagine my delight when visiting Granity on the West Coast last summer to see a sign that offered a WHITEBAIT SAND-WHICH. A local butcher offered ORANIC MEAT for over two years and a Sydenham locksmith is called THREW THE KEYHOLE, apparently not tongue-in-cheek.'

Tim: 'According to the cover of its Business Premier menu, Air New Zealand flies to San Fransisco.' Tony, who works in finance, got personal. He wrote about his former boss. 'I was lightly reprimanded when I granted a small overdraft which she thought was unwarranted. Her comment on the file read, "No further overdraft is to be aloud."' She could probably argue she was offering sound advice.

There were curious similarities in emails from Howard of Auckland and Joyce of Whanganui. Howard wrote: 'Your column reminded me of working on the fit-out of a new shop in Newmarket a few years back. The verandah sign went up: QUALITY PASTERS AND OLIVE'S OILS. I pointed out the errors and the sign was taken down for corrections. Back up later that week, pasters was amended to pastas, but the oils were still Olive's.' Joyce had seen a sign at her local church. It read: TODAY'S SERVICE BY PASTA WILLIAMS: GOD FORGIVES ALL.

Brilliant. But while most readers entered into the proper spirit of celebration, some merely saw an opportunity to bemoan literacy standards. 'Thank you for your column on poor spelling in New Zealand,' Kate wrote. 'Just the other night I found myself following behind a taxi that invited me to call their company on 0800 TAXIS'S. I used to work next to a fish and chip shop that had someone drive through the front of their building. A few days later a sign on their boarded-up window declared: WER'E OPEN.'

So far, so good. I like a rogue apostrophe as much as anyone. But then: 'My brother and I (born and educated in England) despair at the state of the general public's spelling and grammar ability. Ours may not be perfect, but we have found that our abilities far exceed that of the majority of New Zealanders, and we fear it is only going to get worse with the way the current education system is going.'

Oh dear, etc. 'Despair', 'fear' — what about pleasure? There is a good deal of simple fun to be had from witnessing public acts of illiteracy. Can't we just relax and allow ourselves a laugh? No. 'As a member of The Spelling Society, I took particular interest in your column, but would caution you against attaching all the blame on the speller,' Allan emailed. 'Studies show that English spelling makes it much harder for us to learn to read and write than do many other languages (e.g. Italian, Finnish, Korean) which have sensible spelling systems.' He then cited eleven international studies. It was like reading a boring education story in the *Listener*.

Of course, learning difficulties are a serious subject — I sincerely hope last week's Dyslexia Action Week achieved its objectives — and demand sensitivity. How much sensitivity? 'Many, many people are embarrassed at not being able to spell,' wrote Shalagh. Then she told a story. It was a very long story. It had all the solemnity and moral righteousness of a speech by a Rotarian. It described 'a wonderful woman', a charge nurse, who poured her heart and soul into her work at a geriatric ward. 'She would never put anyone down, even when it took four to five baths to get the dirt imbedded from the skin of an elderly bachelor who'd lived in a tank lined with newspapers', etc. Finally, the inevitable remark: 'She could not spell.'

Let us not pass judgment, as Pasta Williams might say. But let us also not pretend to keep a straight face. Generations of Aucklanders have enjoyed the inscription on the Emily Place statue of John Churton, the vicar of St Paul's, who died in 1853. It's a typically long-winded and dull Victorian eulogy. The punchline, though, is pure gold. Where's a 'k' when you need one? The very last sentence reads, 'He rests from his labours, and his wors do follow him.' Pity the poor chiseller; alas, and for our lasting benefit, wors failed him.

[June 28, 2009]

A Flie is Curios

More misspelling in pubic. The most likely culprits are shop signs, menus, that sort of thing. The worse, the merrier. Cheers, then, to Alex of Dunedin, who sent a photograph of a sign advising pub meals in the lovely seaside town of Riverton. The sign reads: LUANCH. He took the photo a few years ago and has heard it's since disappeared. A shame. It belongs in Te Papa. 'I'd like to think,' Alex wrote, 'that the artist is still at work somewhere.'

Me too. It's thrilling to imagine the artist wandering the Earth, intent on mangling the English language in new and ingenious ways. The moving hand writes, and having writ weird nonsense moves on. ... Pam of Wellington reports that the cake section at Pak'nSave in Kilbirnie recently advertised HEART-SHAPED GHETTOES.

Matters of the flesh dominated correspondence from other readers. Carol of unspecified address brings news of her local takeaway offering a sinewy dish called BATTERED MUSCLES. It may or may not come with some fava beans and a nice Chianti.

Jen, also of unspecified address, reports a massive supermarket sign advertising a special on toilet bowl cleaner as

BOWEL CLEANER. Similarly, Jules of Auckland notes that the Nomads Fusion Backpackers hostel in Fort Street offers a BOWEL OF WEDGES.

And, in the same road, Jules claims the Lipstix whorehouse advertises a SPECIAL LUNGERIE NIGHT, although that's probably what it sounds like in a New Zealand accent. Sex tourists who visit our red-light districts must wonder just what girls are talking about when they refer to a lup dunce.

Two readers told stories about correcting misspelled signs. Jacquilyn wrote of an optometrist who set up shop, but the signwriter advertised the business as OPTROMETRIST. 'One of my family members – an ex-teacher who couldn't help herself – pointed out the error, to the optometrist's astonishment. He'd walked past his own window for a not inconsiderable period of time without noticing. He had it corrected in record time.' There are two morals to this story. One: the guy needed glasses. Two: bloody teachers.

Alison of Christchurch wrote, 'I totally agree that we need to celebrate rogue apostrophes and other errors, rather than assuming that they spell the end of the civilised world. I was once wandering around Riccarton when I looked up at the facade of a two-storey building belonging to a monumental masons' and granite importers' company. In big embossed letters, it said (from memory) DECRA ART LTD AND IT'S ASSOCIATES. Since this was a business that engraved tombstones I didn't think it was a good look, so I wrote and pointed it out, stating that I was a member of the grammatical police force, and an unlikely customer of theirs should I need a tombstone engraved.'

And then she quoted the letter in response. 'Thank you for your concern. We were, of course, quite aware of the grammatical error in our sign and had in fact inserted the incorrect apostrophe intentionally, to see how long it would take before some caring soul like yourself brought it to our attention. You are the only person to mention the error since the sign was completed approximately five years ago.

'Now that the game is up, we have removed the offending apostrophe, which you've no doubt already noticed during your vigilant patrols of the area. It's such a great relief to no longer be irritated by it's presence.

'Please accept this small box of chocolates from Decra as the winner of our little competition. Yours faithfully...'

Bravo, John Julian! Also, they were expensive Belgian chocolates.

Errors, accidents and mad inventions keep the English language alive. An email from Peter, however, concerned itself with the end of civilisation. He wrote, badly: 'In the last fifteen years I've spoken with many so-called English language teachers, mostly native New Zealanders, visited many secondary schools, promoting the travel and tourism industry, as a very worthwhile road to follow, for future employment for the pupils. The awful lack of understanding of the English language is very noticeable. On talking with many of these English teachers, it becomes apparent why so many people here are so uneducated...

'I have no qualification in the teaching of English. What I do have is an excellent understanding of the language which was taught to me at school in the 1960s. It wasn't a special school, just a regular grammar school where all students were required to know their own language very well. Conjugation of verbs, syntax, parsing etc were all de rigueur ... I don't see much change for the better in New Zealand in the future, do you?'

Well, I don't see much change for the better in New Zealand in the past. David, a former teacher at Ōmanu Primary School in Mount Maunganui, emailed some of the more outlandish writing assignments from his ex-pupils. 'They suggest,' he wrote, 'that standards forty to fifty years ago were not as universally brilliant as some people claim.'

The most fabulous sample was written by Lynette, aged nine, in 1960. It was about the fly. It reads: 'The flie is a curios anamil it has a row of six fuckers. All down one side.' Bravo, Lynette! I hope she considered a career in signwriting.

[July 19, 2009]

LIFE AND DEATH

Zero Hour

He was once a great athlete. In his youth, he moved like a light breeze on the football grounds of the Bay of Plenty. No one could catch him. The ball was his student. His educated left foot taught it amazing lessons. The willow trees lining the fields of Greerton, Otumoetai and Tauranga crossed their branches and applauded. His performances were legendary, especially in his backyard in Valley Road, Mount Maunganui, where he played his most fabulous games, alone.

The past is another unreliable narrative. It's true that he was as fit as any number of fiddles. In summer, while everyone else flocked to the beach in that seaside town, he practised his skills and ran solitary laps at a deserted park. Even now, years later, there is a faint reminder of his tuned physique as he walks the neighbourhood streets named after birds — Moa, Tui, Kiwi, Huia — to the nearby shops, where he sits at his usual table in the arcade tea room and orders a cup of coffee poured straight from the pot.

He walks at an unhurried pace, but is capable of an explosive burst of pace to skip ahead of dithering old dears in the tea-room queue. He is as slim-hipped as he was in his sporting pomp. He has all his hair. His feet remain delicate instruments.

But they are carrying him ever closer to a destination further away than the shops. They are taking him to a place of no return. They are about to step over a line in the sand. He is headed somewhere barren and cold. Everyone born in a year ending in a zero can keep easy track of their age. His birthday falls on a certain date in the winter of 2010; then and there, he will turn That Age.

That Age is unspeakable. He cannot bring himself to quote the exact number. Enough to say that it ends in a zero, and introduces a void. In a stroke, being That Age renders his entire youth – his childhood, obviously, as well as the teenage years of his athletic prime, but also his gormless twenties and peroxided (what was he thinking?) thirties – ancient history.

Well, he concedes, fair enough. You can't argue with numbers: the year he was born absolutely qualifies as ancient history. In New Zealand (population 2.4 million), Keith Holyoake was re-elected prime minister, and television began. So did the very first episode of *Coronation Street*. In Hamburg, the Indra Club gave a residency to an English music combo called The Beatles. Political news just to hand: JFK has won the US presidential election.

Nothing much else happened. It was the year of the complete knob: famous people who were born then, and who will also turn That Age in 2010, include Bono, Prince Andrew, motivational speaker Tony Robbins, martial arts bonehead Jean-Claude Van Damme, and Mick Hucknall of Simply Red.

Never mind. He has never been particularly aware of the world around him. He has never been particularly aware of anything. Life has passed by in a sometimes fairly pleasant fog. Dreamy at best, dozy at worst, he sets himself the lofty goal of low expectations, and constantly aspires to do things by halves.

A litmus test of New Zealand morality is to account for your whereabouts during the 1981 Springbok tour. He was lurking in an alleyway off Cuba Street, Wellington, as an anti-apartheid protest march tromped down the street. He was having an affair with one of the marchers. They arranged that she would take her place on the outside of the mob. He reached out and grabbed her hand as the protesters chanted, 'Amandla!' He didn't know what the word meant; he thought they were chanting, 'Amanda!' and wished they'd keep their voices down.

His flippant manner ought to help deflect the crisis of turning That Age. He doesn't mind too much the fact that it confirms he's old. He has an old man's tastes – Milk Arrowroot biscuits, Vanilla Wine biscuits, Super Wine biscuits. Nice with a cup of tea. He has an old man's iPod – his carefully selected playlists include swinging hits by mod stars such as Fleetwood Mac, Marc Bolan, 10cc, Rod Stewart, George Michael, Velvet Underground, John Denver. Nice with a cup of tea.

'When you're young,' Martin Amis said in an interview, 'almost the definition of youth is this idea that it's going to last forever, and you're not going to get old like everyone else – it's just a rumour.' What an interesting comment, but he's not sure he felt like that. He was too shy and too vague for the full exuberance of youth. Also, he has been a lifelong misfit. He'll probably be too shy and too vague for the apparent wisdom of old age. Quote from another literary figure, Tom Stoppard: 'Age is a high price to pay for maturity.' He'll pay up on a certain day in the winter of 2010, but he doesn't expect his birthday presents will include the sudden onset of mature thinking.

He has met people much older than That Age who live by a dreary motto: 'Growing old disgracefully.' He doesn't want a bar of that. Their acts of boozed comedy seem so determined, so grim. It's true that now and then he hankers for a drink, by which he means a liquid lunch lasting at least eight hours. But his tremendous thirst is behind him. There were a few lost years, spent in a very pleasant fog, when he could be seen most nights of the week propping up the bar of an upstairs establishment called the Alhambra. He set a record for drinking its house cocktail, The Sigh of the Moor, and later broke it to tell the tale and barely live. He was there, a layabout launching his first book, on the night of 9/11: a sozzled witness to history. He met someone. The planes are the last things he remembers.

It was his happiest decade. He met someone else, and someone else, etc, and toasted his good fortune. By happy chance, the bar closed its doors a month before the birth of his daughter. A father, at last; you do your best living for the love of others. He is now a house cat, an old moggy, domestic and purring, in bed with a beautiful younger woman, sober in charge of a two-year-old. He asks her: 'Am I old?' She says: 'No. You're my daddy.' Good girl. She turns three in February. There'll be balloons, cake, tears, fizz. He turns That Age in June. There'll be tears.

Unconcerned about being old, unbothered that his youth will soon be declared officially kaput, he is nevertheless deeply troubled at the prospect of turning That Age. Is it because the terrible statistic means he'll become, by society's standards, a deadweight, a dead loss, a dead end?

There is a sign above the doorway of That Age. It reads: ABANDON HOPE ALL YE WHO ENTER. Jim White wrote about this in *The Daily Telegraph* last year. He referred to That Age as 'not simply a matter of adding another digit to the chronological scoreboard'. Instead, it meant losing your place as 'part of the 35-plus generation, still thrusting, still upwardly mobile, still someone of potential', and entering 'an entirely new demographic ... the one heading rapidly down a black run to a lonely grave.'

Apart from Winston Peters, no one cares what old people think. White continued: 'Research in the US has indicated that turning [That Age] can be one of life's darkest events.

This is the age that can mark the very trough of life, the basement point in mental well-being, the moment most of us realise that not only have we achieved nothing, but now it's likely we will never achieve anything.'

Yes, that's very cheering. So-called social science research has a habit of bottoming things out. But he doubts he'll mark That Age by squirming inside the very trough of life or crawling around the basement of his mental well-being. He's already been there, done that, a million times. Roll on a quote from another literary figure, Cyril Connolly: 'I have always disliked myself at any given moment. The total of such moments is my life.'

As for the likelihood of never achieving anything – well, all right, that's a shame. But he didn't expect to in the first place. Again with the flippant attitude. Self-effacement is such a tiresome pose. Someone in Paraparaumu once wrote a dismissive review of his first book, and libelled him thus: 'A metropolitan layabout.' How unfair. The truth is that he's always worked hard – in such metropolitan centres as Greymouth, Palmerston North and Te Aroha – to achieve an average result.

He worked long hours even in those lost years at the Al-hambra, although he set up a red couch in his office to sleep off the hangovers. Years earlier, while his contemporaries had saved enough money to whoop it up on a big OE, he worked Monday to Friday as a diligent storeman in a carpet warehouse, and took the train out to various destinations in the Hutt Valley on Saturdays to work as a pedantic sports writer. He wasted his youth on deathless prose: 'Two national records fell to Nelson man Jack Callaghan in yesterday's Cook Strait weightlifting championships held at Naenae.'

It paid off. At thirty, he finally had enough money for a big OE. He returned to Wellington, penniless and dumped by his girlfriend, six weeks later. He signed on to the dole and found a dismal one-bedroom flat. It was beneath an escort agency. The landlord rigged up the telephone lines to share his phone number. He would be woken up at two a.m. by men ringing to inquire about the price of Storm, Roxy and Luna. Sex and money: it sent a message. He moved to Auckland.

Now, as he creeps towards That Age, still determinedly polishing his deathless prose, he is a seasoned professional in his trade and may possibly qualify as an elder statesman. That's a bit grand. Another way of putting it is that he's fast becoming an irrelevance. Actually, he never felt relevant, but he was too young for it to count as an issue. That Age exposes him fair and square.

Already too old for Facebook, Twitter and other ridiculous toys, bored with blogs, personal websites and other blathering vanities, he's behind the times, out of step. He doesn't give a stuff about the tastes of a younger demographic. He's a creature of almost pathological habit – the daily hoof up to the shops along the birding streets of Moa, Tui, Kiwi, Huia. He's very content to be stuck in his ways. Small wonder

That Age is a popular time in all occupations to be shown the door, given the shove, deleted.

But that's not what worries him about turning That Age. He's resilient; he'll survive, probably – someone has to write up the results of the Cook Strait weightlifting championships held at Naenae. That Age presents other, more pressing concerns. The first is that he views the figure as plain embarrassing. It's why he's so coy about naming it. Him, That Age! It's shameful, almost careless, like an accounting error. But the numbers stack up; the sum of their parts is a kind of leprosy. He should be quarantined, kept away from the general public. There goes the long liquid lunch, unless it's held at the RSA.

Yes, yes, he's read all the magazine articles – he wrote one, once – stating that no one acts their age any more, that seventy is the new forty or whatever, but it really doesn't look like that. He gaped with astonishment at the elderly New Zealanders in the studio audience of TV One's execrable New Year's Eve special. They looked exactly like the elderly New Zealanders in the studio audiences of *It's In The Bag* thirty years ago. That Age is the same old That Age.

Yet another quote from a literary figure, partly because he wishes to establish that's the kind of company he wants to be seen in; it wouldn't do to quote Mick Hucknall from Simply Red. George Orwell: 'At [That Age] everyone has the face he deserves.' It's possible to avoid mirrors but other people have to live with it. He feels for his fiancée and his daughter, those captive innocents, as they look across at his crumbling fizzog, day in, day out.

His biggest concern about turning That Age is — naturally, inevitably — its intimation of mortality. Death and that. The final removal, the ultimate fate; off with the light that gleamed an instant, and then endless night. He doesn't much care what it means for himself but others have to live with it. As head of the household, ruler of two vivacious females, his responsibility is to hang on in there as long as possible. He'll very likely give that perhaps not overly flippant consideration on a certain date in the winter of 2010.

This weekend in summer, though, I'll be at another landmark occasion: my brother Paul's sixtieth. The party will be held at the family home in Valley Road, Mount Maunganui. It should be fun. I've always adored Paul. I remember his fiftieth. With our brother, Mark, we stayed up drinking all night, and cleared away the hangovers with a brisk stumble to the beach in the morning. The light was clean and clear over the horizon.

[January 10, 2010]

Cemetery Road

Where is New Zealand's best cemetery? The most picturesque, the loveliest, sweetest, saddest? Ideally the dead would vote, but they're too lazy. Death in New Zealand resides in about four hundred estates. A great many were established in the nineteenth century. 'Every town and small settlement in New Zealand has an old cemetery,' writes Stephen Deed, author of *Unearthly Landscape*s. He argues that old cemeteries are 'the repositories of family and community histories, and should be treasured as part of our heritage.'

That, and they look really great. The light, the shade, the low metal gate; the trimmed lawn, the glass jam jar filled with wilting plastic flowers. Now and then a crypt to store a stiff on the ground floor, rather than in the basement; sometimes a sensational angel, flying nowhere fast. But the chances are good that you'll only ever see once in your life the likes of the thing that dominates the cemetery at West Taieri, near Mosgiel. It's a great big red box. Beneath it, or possibly rattling around somewhere inside it, is Elizabeth Joseph, who died in 1882 – strange to think of a great big red box sitting there, weird and squat, for over a century.

It's a pretty little graveyard; possibly, even, the prettiest in New Zealand. The light, the shade, the bellbirds. Daniel Heenan, who died in 1898, makes a vain but impressive bid to compete with Elizabeth Joseph's sarcophagus with his grave, a massive, finely detailed cathedral. Despite its great size it looks like a doll's house, a miniature replica of some actual church. Magpies survey the cemetery from the highest spire.

The dead are eyeless. But there are magnificent views — possibly, even, the best in New Zealand — from the cemetery in Bluff. It looks over Foveaux Strait, and upon Stewart Island. It's a record of shipping news. The headstones read: Andrew King, drowned 1894; Arthur Lightfoot, drowned 1913; Bernard Lovett, drowned 1915; Erasmus Duncan, drowned 1942; there's also a monument, in the shape of a great big rock, dedicated to Bluff's founder, James Spencer. It reads: 'Died at sea. 1846.'

William Hobson, New Zealand's founding governor, opened Auckland's downtown Symonds Street Cemetery in 1842. He visited again in September that year: dead at forty-nine. In a previous column I described his grave as 'nothing upstanding, no statue, no bust, just a slab of concrete hemmed in by a short rail fence, with three black rubbish bags caught on the spikes'. Disrepair is everywhere, including among the living: the cemetery is a favoured hideaway for drunks and glue-sniffers, and it's also where serial prisoner escaper Kevin Polwart was arrested in February, when police found him wearing a not especially discreet yellow fluorescent jacket. But the 'shaded lanes, the daffodils in spring, the oaks and birds and stiff Anglican sentiment' at Symonds Street give the cemetery a dreamily English feel; possibly, even, the most English in New Zealand.

Wellington's downtown Bolton Street Cemetery may be New Zealand's grandest. There are olde roses and iron monuments and a cool, quiet walkway that leads to the botanic garden. Here lies Seddon, Wakefield, Turnbull and other distinguished etceteras. There are dead famous, too, at St Mary's charming hillside cemetery – possibly, even, New Zealand's most charming hillside cemetery – in New Plymouth. The gravestone of Charles Armitage Brown reads: FRIEND OF KEATS. Brown had been a mentor to the poet. He sailed from England to New Plymouth in 1841. He died the following year 'after a brief but outspoken residence in the new settlement'. And one of the most famous names in the entire world can be found in the Hokianga's Kohukohu Cemetery, where a plain white wooden cross announces the death in 1963 of John Lennon.

It's false and complacent to think of cemeteries as unsullied. Because the number one social problem in New Zealand is profound boredom, vandals and various assorted mongs will always attack a graveyard. It's something to do, and undo. Recent targets include Rimu Cemetery in Christchurch, Aramoho Cemetery in Whanganui (last August, an attempt was made to set alight the grave of murdered woman Tania

McKenzie), Kauae Cemetery in Ngongotaha (six headstones were trashed the day before Sir Howard Morrison's funeral), and Nelson's Marsden Valley Cemetery is in a sorry state since thieves ran off last month with bronze grave markers to sell for scrap metal.

Custodians must remain vigilant. Civic pride is at stake. Dunedin, properly, bangs on about its historic 'story-telling' Northern Cemetery, which claims the bones of Larnach and Speight. Waikumete, in Auckland, is New Zealand's largest cemetery, home to over 70,000 phantoms. Features of this sprawling estate include unmarked graves of victims of the 1918 influenza epidemic, and a mass grave containing unidentified passengers who died on Mount Erebus.

It's likely, though, that New Zealand's best cemetery is rural. Is it at Ormond, Dipton, Redhill, Burkes Pass, Colville or Ross? Is it at Mataura, Kaponga, Purakanui, Hira, Puketapu or Te Kapa? Somewhere quiet and small, a place of Māori and migrant, verse and dates, birds and falling leaves, within a tender zone of disappearance.

[March 7, 2010]

George Best's Birthday

He died in 2005. He was fifty-nine. The wonder of it is that he lived so long. It was as though he kept a suicide note tucked in his pocket for thirty years. As a professional alcoholic – he was paid to be famous and he was famous because he was a drunk – he worked very hard to drink himself to death. A liver transplant saved his life in 2002, and he was thankful it gave him a second chance, but he returned to the certainty of alcohol. It killed him. He got his death wish.

I heard about it by text. It read: 'Best dead.' I have to look up the date of his death, but I know the date of his birth off by heart: May 22. He would have turned sixty-four yesterday. What do you do on the birthday of someone who's dead? You remember their life.

George Best was a football player. I was a fan. The two scrapbooks of newspaper clippings, the fourteen books about him stacked up on my desk – it ought to be childish, a quaint and harmless exercise in mere nostalgia, but the pages document a hard, desolate character. Interview, 1969: 'I don't really need other people all that much.' Interview, 1987: 'They'll never get to me. They'll never get to that part of me that matters.' He was the keeper of a secret: his genius, which made him the most exciting and naturally gifted football player in history. 'People want to understand genius but they can't.'

He craved company, and wanted to be left alone. In his great and devastating study of Best, novelist Gordon Burn wrote about his final years as a quiet, bleary sot, pinned to the corner of his local pub with a pint glass of wine, his shoulders salted with dandruff, peering over his glasses as he solved the *Daily Mirror* crossword puzzle. When he was in his pomp in 1968 as the most celebrated footballer in Britain, an ex-girlfriend said, 'He sticks to things he knows.' That was Burn's thesis too. Best was born in Belfast. His father worked in the shipyards. Burn wrote: 'Best ended up drinking in the company of a woman called Gina in a council house that was a dirty version – gerbils in a cage in the bath, the reek of cats – of the one he had grown up in.'

Shelter from a storm. What storm? That was another secret no one ever knew. His club, Manchester United, sent him to a psychiatrist. Burn described him as 'an easily worried creature'; another biographer, Joe Lovejoy, wrote of his 'tormented eyes'. One of his oldest friends told Lovejoy, 'I don't think he's a happy man. Don't ask me what the root of it is because I don't know. The way his mother died, perhaps.' Ann Best became an alcoholic after her son, but did a quicker job of it; she died in 1978. One of his sisters has battled with alcoholism. Best told Michael Parkinson in an amazing book they wrote together, 'Sometimes I sit and think where it really all went wrong.'

He never solved that puzzle. He was an enigma wrapped around a bottle of vodka. The two scrapbooks and the fourteen books illustrate a standard narrative arc – genius and madness, rise and fall. He played out both stories on his two visits to New Zealand. He came here with Manchester United in 1967; they beat Auckland 8–1 and New Zealand 11–0. His manager, Matt Busby, later wrote of Best's performance in the Auckland game: 'It was one of the most incredible displays I have ever seen. Every time he got the ball this New Zealander behind me said in a loud and sorrowful voice, "Oh my God, he's got it again. What's he going to do this time?" That's what I shall remember about George.'

Best returned in 1996 on a speaking tour. His fall had rolled him downhill to a hall in Te Rapa, in front of seventy people, and Tauranga, where the audience was only forty-nine. I met him in Auckland. I remember his anxious, rapidly blinking eyes, his light voice, his fat hands. But I also remember his wit. He was a very funny man. The conventional George Best story is told as tragedy. It could be worse – a theatre in Belfast is about to produce a musical based on his life – but it fails to allow for the fact that much of the George Best story is comedy.

A deep foundation of laughter always lay beneath his nihilism. He knew how to have a good time. He wallowed in pleasure. 'It was like the last days of Rome,' he said, lasciviously, about most of his days. His genius was for happiness. In 1970, a match report in the *The Guardian* described a goal he scored against Chelsea: 'Twice Harris tried to bring him down from behind and twice Best eluded him. Best next rounded the goalkeeper, stopped briefly to have a chat with Harris, who had appeared abruptly, and then tapped the ball into the net. Insolence gone mad!'

I love that exclamation mark. I acknowledge his commitment to oblivion. Genius and madness, rise and fall; the arc stops at his death. But I retrace it every year on May 22, when I remember his birthday.

[May 23, 2010]

My Birthday

She asked, 'Are you a teenager, Dad?' But that was last week, when I was young as summer, and today I am fifty. The clocks are too tired to tick, the tide is shuffling out the door. I reach down through the ages and stroke my daughter's blonde hair. At three, she shines like a new coin. All children get from room to room by running; she gets from room to room by running, all motion, her silly limbs disappearing into her bedroom to find a doll, a sheet of stickers, a jar of buttons. Her games have set rules, strict terms. 'Okay. You lie there,' she commands, and points to the carpet. Good. Deliver me unto dust and lint. I am static, an old warhorse. Earlier this month, I put in my request for birthday presents from her beautiful mother: a dressing gown, and slippers. Tartan would be nice.

The day of the dread has arrived. Numbers are so absolute: 50 is 50, and a feeble blast of the whistle announces the second half of life is about to kick off. The first half had its moments. There were my delicate twenties, my drunk thirties, my dubious forties. And now? 'He sailed,' W.H. Auden wrote of Herman Melville's later years, 'into an extraordinary mildness.' I've always loved that line. I think I've always waited and even longed for it to happen.

A recent *Listener* magazine cover caught my attention when it ordered: LIVE TO BE 100. I thought: oh fuck off. Another fifty years, wheezing, aching, forgetting, hoarding, taking up space – better to cut the second half short. But the final descent of those senior years and senior moments, with the bus pass and the rattling teacup, the toenails as hard as tortoise shells and the mind as soft as a three-minute boiled egg, feels like a long way off. It is a long way off. At fifty, it exists as fiction, as something only imagined, like death.

I lead an active life. I read, I write. I once stepped into a gym. It looked like an unpleasant and ridiculous place, and I stepped out for a cigarette. No doubt a regime of physical suffering would yield results and do me some good, but I doubt I could deal with the shame. I have always tried to live according to the highest principles of distaste for the goal of self-improvement. No sense in betraying those ideals now.

I suppose there are other, easier ways to express panic. I could start dressing differently. Every city in New Zealand has a clothes shop selling younger apparel for the older gentleman. It's a chain store called Younger Apparel for the Older Gentleman. Or I could shave my head, and grow a beard. Or I could go the whole desperate hog and get a tattoo, but I already have one. It's inked in shadows all over my face. It reads: FIFTY.

You're only as old as you feel. I feel contempt for that cliché. Children keep you young. More nonsense, although it's true I slept like a baby the other day when I took an afternoon nap on my daughter's bed. She is so lovely, so adorable and fascinating; at fifty, the savage need to watch her grow up means that I have to look after myself almost as much as I look after her. I should stop smoking. Strange to think that when I'm eligible for a pension is when it's legal for her to buy alcohol. We could go out and celebrate over a drink. Her shout.

Today, too, is a celebration. Fifty: got there, made it. I always figured I would expire in ludicrous circumstances – a piano pushed from an apartment window at the exact time I was minding my own business on the pavement, that sort of thing. Probably the only time I came close to death was when I absent-mindedly walked into the crater of a semi-active volcano in Indonesia and fell, landing on my back on a ledge a few metres above a bed of red spluttering lava, but it all turned out all right, thanks to a man with a very long cord of rope attached to his donkey.

There are worse fates than death. Many of us reach fifty but have surrendered to madness, despair or bitterness. A kind of smugness is acceptable. My life has turned out very much all right at fifty. No donkey required; love always rescues, and it binds me tight to the two girls in our house strewn with dolls, stickers, buttons. I have books to finish reading and writing; curiosity keeps me locked up inside the house of language strewn with images, sentences, chapter headings.

Sooner or later we all get to THE END, but fifty is MTC. I remember typing newspaper stories back when the practice was that they had to be written on small sheets of paper. The formula dictated that one sheet of paper equalled one paragraph. Until the story was finished, you had to write a code on the bottom right-hand corner of each page: MTC. More to come. Hopefully. Fifty: this way lies mildness. From today, I go out on the tide, tattooed and ancient, slippered and loved, moreish.

[June 20, 2010]

ACKNOWLEDGEMENTS

My thanks to *The Sunday-Star Times*; Tranz Scenic Rail;
Waikato Institute of Technology; the trustees of the Buddle
Findlay Sargeson Fellowship; Matt Vance at Antarctica
New Zealand; Coco's Café, Point Chevalier; writers
Neil Cross, Anthony McCarten and Charlotte Grimshaw;
readers Peter Gow, Robin Beckinsale, and James Alexander
Heath-Caldwell; and Mary Varnham and Sarah Bennett
at Awa Press.

How to Watch a Bird
Steve Braunias
978-0-9582629-6-5

'Braunias's wit and charm are put to work to explain in
easy non-scientific ways why looking at the commonest
birds can be such a pleasure'
The Dominion Post: Best Non-Fiction of 2007

**Prize-winning journalist Steve Braunias is standing on the balcony
of an inner-city apartment on a sultry summer evening when a
black-backed gull flies so close he is instantaneously bowled over
with happiness. 'I thought: Birds, everywhere. I want to know more
about them.' This highly engaging book is the result – a personal
journey into an amazing world. It's also a New Zealand history, a
geographical wandering, and an affectionate look at the tribe of
people ensnared, captivated and entranced by birds.**

'Braunias has touchingly brought love and bird-watching together in a book
that stalks sewage ponds and grey warblers with curiosity and affection,
and ends with contentment, bliss and a baby born. A lovely book'
New Zealand Listener: Best Books of 2007

'A small and perfectly formed jewel'
The Sunday Star-Times

'Awa Press plus Braunias plus birds makes for a tantalising
literary marriage'
New Zealand Life & Leisure

Available from all good bookstores and online at
www.awapress.com

By the same author

Roosters I Have Known
Steve Braunias
978-0-9582750-5-7

'Classic Steve Braunias – provocative, literate, disrespectful and eminently readable ... some of the best writing you will read this winter'
Christopher Moore, *The Press*

In 2007 Steve Braunias embarked on a series of 27 interviews, one a week, profiling New Zealanders famous and infamous, both publicity-seekers and those desperate to hide from the spotlight. His startling survey of the national psyche ranged from the neuro-scientist Richard Faull to rape survivor Louise Nicholas, from actor Adam Rickitt to TV star Paul Henry, from Cuisine's Julie Dalzell to Fox Television's Anita McNaught in Iraq. He also took us to our leaders – Labour's Helen Clark, National's John Key, the Māori Party's Pita Sharples ... and a miscellany of mayoral wannabes. You may never vote again.

'Braunias proves that he is our best newspaper feature writer'
Warwick Roger, *North & South*

'Opinionated, prickly, sometimes fevered, often affectionate – cranky vintage Braunias'
Lindsey Dawson, *Plenty*

'Funny, touching, smart ... Recommended'
Sam Finnemore, *Craccum*

Available from all good bookstores and online at
www.awapress.com

Fish of the Week
Steve Braunias
978-0-9582750-6-4

'If you are ever feeling blue, read one of these delicious essays.
The sun will soon shine again … Every one is a gem'
Graham Beattie, *Beattie's Book Blog*

Steve Braunias's satirical and closely observed writings have
driven readers to drink, God, lawyers, and sometimes to the shops
to shower him with gifts. In this lascivious selection he addresses the
state of New Zealand steak, the beauty of mangroves, the lunacy of
film festivals, the attractions of small towns ('There is no statistic that
says a village can accommodate only one village idiot'), the charms
of Cambridge University and the strange habits of the English,
and more – as well as his own intimate, seesawing, surprisingly
vulnerable life as a writer and lovestruck father.

'Diverse, whimsical, clever … absolutely recommended'
Sonja de Friez, *Radio New Zealand Nine to Noon*

'Braunias has intelligently wormed his way into my heart, stirred me with his
gentle eloquence, bowled me with his wit … damn funny and insightful'
Matt Rilkoff, *Taranaki Daily News*

'A brilliant and eccentric collection'
Philip Matthews, *Your Weekend*